Splendid Failure

SPLENDID FAILURE

Postwar Reconstruction in the American South

Michael W. Fitzgerald

The American Ways Series

IVAN R. DEE   *Chicago*

www.ivanrdee.com

Library of Congress Cataloging-in-Publication Data:
Fitzgerald, Michael W., 1956–
    Splendid failure : postwar Reconstruction in the American South / Michael W. Fitzgerald.
        p. cm. (American ways series)
    Includes index.
    ISBN- 13: 978-1-56663-734-3 (cloth : alk. paper)
    ISBN- 10: 1-56663-734-1 (cloth : alk. paper)
    ISBN- 13: 978-1-56663-739-8 (pbk. : alk. paper)
    ISBN- 10: 1-56663-739-2 (pbk. : alk. paper)
    1. Reconstruction (U.S. history, 1865–1877). 2. United States—Politics and government—1865–1877. 3. Republican Party (U.S. : 1854–)—History—19th century. 4. Southern States—Politics and government—1865–1950. 5. Southern States—Race relations—History—19th century. 6. Southern States—Social conditions—1865–1945. 7. Southern States—Economic conditions—19th century. I. Title.
E668.F54 2007
973.8—dc22

2006100487

To my sons, Alex and Nate

Contents

Preface

FOR GENERATIONS the memory of Reconstruction was among the most contentious in American life; it long remained associated with matters of pressing concern. At the turn of the twentieth century, professional historians used the presumed excesses of Reconstruction to defend Jim Crow, disfranchisement, even lynching. The dominant "Columbia" school of William A. Dunning and his students depicted Republican Reconstruction as an exercise in fanaticism and corruption. After mid-century, another generation of scholars recoiled from this racist version. Amid the inspiring events of the civil rights era, revisionists swept the field. Historians now saw Reconstruction as a laudable attempt to ensure basic equality for the former slaves. In recent decades serious scholarship has proceeded from these premises, criticizing Republican Reconstruction, if anything, for being insufficiently drastic. The dominant modern synthesis of the field, Eric Foner's brilliant *Reconstruction: America's Unfinished Revolution*, places the legitimate social and political aspirations of African Americans at the center of the narrative.

In the early twenty-first century the popular interest in Reconstruction generated by the 1960s struggles has waned. Perhaps the time is opportune for a reconsideration of the era. This book pursues the field's implicit comparison with the civil rights movement, but in a different direction: A century after Reconstruction, Martin Luther King and his comrades were able to galvanize national opinion and force federal intervention. The attitude of the Northern public was the determining factor, and the nonviolent movement brilliantly used the media to dramatize the justice of its cause. This raises the issue of why the earlier proponents of racial justice failed, why they were unable to sustain the kind of Northern support they needed. One would think that after a bloody Civil War, Northerners would protect their late black allies from those who had recently risen in rebellion. They had the strongest possible motives to keep racist Democrats from reassuming power. Yet these former Confederates prevailed, through fraud and violence and in obvious violation of the laws, while the public chose to look away.

This book examines how the proponents of racial justice lost the support they needed. What they did may not have ultimately mattered, given the underlying state of national sentiment; as the passions of the war dissipated, perhaps nothing could have sustained egalitarian commitments. The limitations posed by Northern opinion are evident throughout this book. Still, one can argue that Reconstruction's supporters squandered assets unnecessarily, given their fragile lease on Northern sympathy. Professor Foner puts African-American agency at the center of his narrative, as does this work, but with somewhat different results. I argue that Republican leaders, both white and black, eased the capitulation of national opinion to white supremacy, in ways that should have been foreseeable. An exploration of their choices, amid such difficult circumstances, may illuminate more modern alternatives as we seek a better world.

Acknowledgments

IN ATTEMPTING to write a broad synthesis of an era, one accumulates a great many intellectual debts. Several colleagues at a distance were kind enough to read the manuscript. I would like to thank John Rodrigue, Margaret Washington, and Christopher Waldrep for reading drafts on short notice. Mark Summers read and instantly critiqued the manuscript at exhaustive length, and he has my grateful thanks. Finally, my fourteen-year-old son Nate was kind enough to read the manuscript, providing novel insights.

I thank my colleagues in the history department at St. Olaf College for general intellectual support, and the institution itself for a generous sabbatical policy. The interlibrary loan librarians at St. Olaf—Kasia Gonnerman, Sara Leake, and Jill Engle— have been uniformly helpful. More broadly, I have been able to teach consistently in such fields as African-American and Southern history in ways that furthered the intellectual gestation of the project. As I write this, the students in my Civil War class are reading the draft as one of my course textbooks. Students are pelting me with writing advice on a daily basis. One seldom gets such immediate feedback on one's work, and I am thankful for their coerced assistance.

Finally, I thank my wife and departmental colleague, Judy Kutulas, and my other son, Alex. The project is theirs as much as mine, and I am deeply grateful.

M. W. F.

Northfield, Minnesota
March 2007

"If the Reconstruction of the Southern states . . . had been conceived as a major national program of America, whose accomplishment at any price was well worth the effort, we should be living today in a different world. . . . The attempt to make black men American citizens was in a certain sense all a failure, but a splendid failure."
—W. E. B. Du Bois

Splendid Failure

1

To Civil War: What Slavery Did

FROM THE VANTAGE POINT of the early twenty-first century, the surprising thing about Reconstruction is not that it failed. The striking thing is that a serious attempt to establish racial equality was made at all. Given the centrality of slavery in the nation's previous history, and the strength of white supremacy as a dominant value, only a bloody Civil War could have put legal equality on the national agenda. How that war came about had much to do with the institution of slavery and what it did to the South and the nation. Slavery is the starting point for understanding the era's transformations.

One could go far back to trace the origins of the war, to the beginnings of slavery and the notions of racial hierarchy it spawned. Or, on a more positive note, one might talk about the democratic aspirations of the American Revolution. But for our purposes the solidification of the cotton kingdom will suffice. The cotton gin made that crop the raw material for textile production, cloth being the first mass-produced commodity of the Industrial Revolution. Over the course of the nineteenth century the South would produce half or more of the world's cotton, and fortunes could be made in the Western domain being wrested from the Native Americans. The crop swept across fertile lands from South Carolina to eastern Texas. In the Deep South

planters made fine returns growing cotton, while in the Upper
South slaveholders profited by raising human beings for sale. An
institution that had looked moribund revived, providing quick
fortunes and social mobility for multitudes of whites. Profit dis-
placed the Jeffersonian talk of phasing out slavery, but this put
the region out of step in a wider European-dominated world and
its conceptions of progress.

Southern society assumed the shape and manifested the divisions that would later become so crucial. One aspect is the evolution of the enslaved population after the slave trade ended. As
imported Africans gave way to African-American slaves, they
learned English and became less foreign to whites culturally. In
particular, the mass conversion of slaves to the Baptist and
Methodist churches provided a common evangelical language
that some whites took seriously. Although these churches' initial
anti-slavery inclination ebbed after the Revolution, they drew
numbers of slaves to a socially sanctioned doctrine subject to
multiple interpretations. Christianity shielded political discussion in the slave quarters; it provided a democratic cultural re-
source to express a veiled critique of the institution. Throughout
the antebellum decades, slaves suffered forced relocation westward that shattered ties of family and community. Still, it became more possible for masters to substitute unequal bargaining
for brute force. Give and take was possible as long as the threat
of force or sale was sufficiently vivid.

These realities were everywhere. Even after emancipation,
the Confederate general Josiah Gorgas wrote of the "inevitable
big whip of an overseer or small planter." Violence was essential.
In the 1790s slaveholders saw the successful rebellion in Haiti (or
Santo Domingo). The French revolutionary slogans of Liberty,
Equality, Fraternity reverberated dangerously in slave colonies.
In America, Fourth of July rhetoric and Bible texts could be put
to unanticipated uses, and so could slave and free blacks' increas-

ing literacy and savvy. In 1822 members of a slave congregation in Charleston were at least talking insurrection; one idea was to seize the ships in the harbor and escape to liberated Haiti. Officials took Denmark Vesey's plot seriously enough to execute thirty-five people. In 1831 came the ultimate nightmare, the slave preacher Nat Turner's insurrection which killed some sixty white men, women, and children in Southampton County, Virginia. Thereafter whites needed to look no farther to have their fears dramatized in blood.

Ambitious plots always failed. Perhaps two hundred slaves died in the disorderly aftermath of Turner's rebellion alone. The upshot was legislation controlling free blacks and discouraging emancipation, laws restricting slave mobility, literacy, and unsupervised religious activity. Slaveholders also redoubled their efforts to propagate the right Gospel, the one that sanctioned servitude. In the face of all this, most slaves concluded that craft or manipulation worked better than revolt. Running away, theft, poor work, and the South's constant arson problem were ubiquitous. Some slaves probably just tried not to think about the limitations of their lives, others awaited divine deliverance. They fantasized about freedom all the time and talked about it occasionally, but under normal circumstances collective resistance was suicide.

Perhaps this conclusion is too facile. A lawyer asked Nat Turner if his defeat didn't prove he was wrong. "Was not Christ crucified?" came Turner's response, suggesting that martyrdom could yield positive consequences. His rebellion, combined with the rising international criticism of slavery, encouraged drastic measures. Raw emotions guaranteed that when a political threat materialized, the Deep South response would be vigorous. A slaveholder's revolution risked everything, but this was a difficult case for skeptics to make in a climate of fear. The slave conspirators thus arguably succeeded. Rebellions prodded the master class toward a jumpy resort to secession, which would demolish the social order overnight.

Beyond the growing knowledge of the slaves in Euro-American culture, and their increasingly sophisticated resistance, other changes took place. Increasing occupational, and what one might call status, differentiation occurred. As one former slave recalled, "De fust class was de house servants. Dese was de butler, de maids, de nurses, chambermaids, and de cooks. De nex' class was de carriage drivers and de gardeners, de carpenters, de barber and de stable men. . . . De lowest class was de common field niggers." Most slaves remained field hands, but some men moved into supervisory positions as drivers. Growing numbers picked up marketable skills that would let them work as craftsmen, sometimes even renting their own time from their masters. Domestics gained considerable familiarity with their oppressor's culture, particularly access to literacy.

In 1860, 10 percent of the black population were free nationwide. Some had escaped to the North, some were freed formally. Still others came to an informal arrangement with nominal owners. Individual prodigies of labor or sheer luck liberated people; Denmark Vesey had won his freedom in a lottery. Liberation also resulted from some relationships between white men and slave women. However one evaluates the murky combination of coercion and emotion involved, some men freed their enslaved lovers and children. Especially in the Deep South, free blacks were described in the census as disproportionately "mulatto" rather than black, and property ownership was significantly correlated with lighter skin color.

Concentrated in the region's few cities, the population of legally free or quasi-slave African Americans often prospered. The most conspicuously privileged population was the "Creoles" of the Gulf Coast, their station reflecting the long Latin acceptance of interracial liaisons. Locally they were considered something of an intermediate racial category, a status reflected in treaty obligations with France and Spain. They often inherited substantial sums; in 1830 some 146 free people of color owned five or more slaves in New Orleans alone. In eight parishes in the Louisiana countryside, 43 nonwhite planters owned more than 1,300 slaves. The Creoles, and free blacks more broadly, enjoyed educational advantages that were unlike those of the mass of slaves. One Yankee novelist, John De Forest, compared Louisiana's Creoles to "white negroes from the Mountains of the Moon." Their social loyalties were complex, but when emancipation eliminated their protected niche they provided much of the Reconstruction leadership.

If slavery generated a black elite, it also generated a baseline democratic solidarity among the enslaved masses. The field hands, predominantly darker-skinned, shared common experiences and grievances; all knew what it meant to have men, women, and children working in the fields, generally under the whip. They lived together in the slave quarters, ate the same food, and evaded the same patrollers. They relied on one another to shield their various infractions against authority. And, of course, they all faced the same threat of sale. The specifics of slavery inevitably colored their conception of freedom. As the wartime spiritual gleefully intoned, "No more auction block for me. . . . No more peck of corn for me. . . . No more driver's lash for me. . . ." The list went on and on. Freedpeople would confront baffling new realities, but they knew what to avoid.

If slavery shaped the African-American population, it equally influenced the master race. The rise of the cotton kingdom solidified social hierarchy in much the form it would take by the time of the Civil War. Across the Deep South, commercial production dominated the fertile river valleys and the great central plantation belt. The crops varied: plantations grew short-staple cotton in most of the Deep South, with sugar in southern

Louisiana and rice and luxury long-staple cotton in coastal South
Carolina and Georgia. Tobacco dominated in the Upper South,
increasingly supplemented by grain—and always by the sale of
human property south and west. The specifics differed, but plantation production for market was the constant. The scale of the
financial investment was vast. In 1860 a prime male slave was
worth approximately $1,800, about $40,000 in modern terms.
Since slaves represented about one-third of the Southern population, the investment was colossal—billions of dollars. For the
fourth of white families that owned slaves, concentrated in the
plantation regions, this was an overriding reality. When the crisis
came, the plantation areas would back the Confederacy with the
greatest conviction.

Elsewhere things were different. On poorer lands and areas
away from easy transportation of goods, slavery was not as pervasive. White population concentrated in such areas, especially in
the highlands of Appalachia or the Ozarks, and in less fertile areas elsewhere. Family farms producing food crops predominated. One historian conceptualized the antebellum South as a
"dual economy," having both a rich plantation region and an upland periphery with only limited market involvement. Upland
farmers were not entirely isolated; they produced livestock and
drove it to market. Slaves worked in the fertile river valleys of
Appalachia, and even in the highlands slaveholders dominated
elective office. Still, the upland South *was* different, with its limited stake in slavery and physical and intellectual isolation.

Daniel Hundley reflected on these issues on the eve of war, in
his *Social Relations in Our Southern States*. He stressed the unity
of Southern slaveholders and upwardly mobile farmers in the
plantation belt and surrounding piedmont. He sharply distinguished this wholesome majority from those he termed "Poor
White Trash," clustered in the hilly and mountainous regions.
Living in log cabins, clad in homespun, they lived by barter and

drank bad liquor. Hundley thought them morally inferior to the slaves, perhaps even by blood. The future Klan leader Randolph Shotwell described North Carolina's mountain people in almost identical terms, as a "distinct race of people . . . thriftless, uneducated, unthinking beings, who live little better than negroes. . . ." One suspects the hill folk saw themselves differently, and these social divisions played out during the sectional controversy.

Upland farmers resented elite pretensions. This sense of difference was sometimes reflected in indirect ways. In the antebellum decades the powerful Baptist church was shaken by internal debates. Historically the Baptists had been a frontier faith, decentralized and respectful of those of modest means and education. As the Baptists rose to regional influence, prosperous members pursued the improvement initiatives common during the Jacksonian era, like temperance, Sunday schools, distribution of Bibles, and other efforts to spread enlightenment. This evoked an "anti-Mission" backlash, primarily in backwoods areas away from the plantation belt and cities. Primitive Baptist churches spread, emphasizing old-fashioned predestination along with entire autonomy for congregations. This sort of touchy localism encouraged resistance to secession, and even in the Deep South these congregations were often centers of dissent.

Political rivalries between the plantation regions and the up-country reflected this sense of difference. Superimposed on this pattern was the national party system, which solidified in the 1830s and 1840s as a rivalry between Jacksonian Democrats, who preferred small government and vigorous westward expansion, and their Whig opponents, who preferred a strong central government that could foster commerce. The configuration differed in response to local interests, but in the Deep South rich planters and urban elites tended to align with the Whig party. The highlanders were more strongly drawn to the localism and low taxes promoted by the Democrats—as well as the rowdy personal style of President Andrew Jackson, the dominant politician of the era. The North Carolina Unionist William W. Holden recalled that Whigs lived "mainly in the towns and villages" while his fellow Democrats were "in the eye of society, ignorant and awkward."

Rivalry between the Whigs and Democrats did not translate directly into Reconstruction divisions; the white Republican minority came from both. Most future Republicans resisted the states' rights Democratic tendency, but otherwise they had little in common ideologically. Still, these partisan debates highlight antebellum political fissures, which were most charged along lines of region and class. Where Unionist politics reinforced these earlier divisions, they were most powerful. Few upland farmers questioned white supremacy, which made them problematic eventual allies for the freedmen, but the institution of servitude itself mattered less to them. When the war came, this reality transformed existing political loyalties.

As sectional controversy heated up after the Mexican War, older political loyalties based on economic and constitutional issues grew strained. The crisis strengthened the Democrats, with their states' rights and pro-Southern tilt, while it undermined the Whig preference for an expansive federal government and sectional moderation. The emergence in the mid-1850s of a Northern anti-slavery party, the Republicans, and the confrontations over the question of slavery in the Western territories inflamed Southern opinion, as did John Brown's attempted insurrection at Harpers Ferry. In the election of 1860 the Republican Abraham Lincoln pledged to restrict slavery's spread while his opposition splintered. The states' rights Democrats nominated John Breckinridge, who carried the Deep South. Against him ran the national Democrat Stephen Douglas and also the former Whig John Bell, who between them dominated the Upper South. Their following was often lumped together terminologically as "Conservatives," as opposed to the sectional extremism suggested by the Breckinridge candidacy. The modest Douglas contingent was especially identified with Unionist views, having broken with its Southern Democratic comrades over the issue of sectional extremism.

When Lincoln carried the free states and won, South Carolina precipitated the final showdown by seceding. Popular alarm bolstered the immediate secessionists, making it difficult to urge caution without being tarred as a "submissionist." Secessionist emissaries spread a nightmare vision of Republican rule. One warned of consigning Southern daughters "to pollution and violation to gratify the lust of half-civilized Africans." Another predicted political equality, which meant "black governors, black legislatures, black juries, black everything." These overwrought fears made effective rhetoric, but they would be difficult to shake when emancipation and equal suffrage became reality.

Most whites in the Deep South saw disunion as necessary after Lincoln's election. Still, the secession votes were often close, with a large "cooperationist" minority in most states favoring an ill-defined collaborative response: maybe unified secession, perhaps an ultimatum first, or possibly just delay. Opposition to immediate secession coalesced from two distinct sources. Slaveholding former Whigs were mostly silenced by events, but in the wealthiest plantation areas, like central Georgia or the great Mississippi river counties of Louisiana and Mississippi, cooperationists generally won. A more determined opposition to secession was evident in the up-country areas in northern Alabama and Georgia. In these areas, traditionally dominated by Democrats, immediate secessionists lost badly. Cooperationist votes thus seem to have meant different things in different places. Among the Whiggish planters they expressed disagreement over how best to protect slavery. In the mountains the huge margins represented more—a disinclination to secede that shaded into Unionism. Intransigent opponents, clustered in such areas, became the Deep South's premier white outsiders, cut adrift from dominant opinion over the coming war.

Unionism was stronger in the Upper South, where slavery was less pervasive. After Lincoln's election, eight slave states rejected secession for the time being. While disunion had support in the plantation districts, elsewhere it was buried. But much of this sentiment was conditional, favoring the status quo as long as the federal government refrained from coercion. In April 1861 the new Confederate government under President Jefferson Davis forced the issue by firing on Fort Sumter. Four remaining slave states—Kentucky, Maryland, Missouri, and Delaware—found themselves on the front line of a Union war against fellow slaveholders, having to choose sides. Four more states—Virginia, Tennessee, Arkansas, and North Carolina—instead joined the Confederacy.

Even before fighting began, many former opponents of secession acquiesced, hoping that a show of Southern unity might deter invasion. When war broke out, most concluded that the die was cast. Volunteering was brisk, and throughout 1861 Confederate victories rallied popular support. Still, pockets of opposition remained, especially in the mountains. The western counties of Virginia rejected secession, welcoming Union troops and eventually forming a separate state. In highland east Tennessee, months after Fort Sumter, the electorate still voted two to one against secession. An uprising occurred in anticipation of Union invasion, prompting public hangings and widespread arrests.

The Davis administration initially commanded widespread support, but this sentiment was more conditional outside the plantation regions, which rallied to the Confederacy. Secessionists had promised either peaceful separation or a short, decisive war. One leader actually offered to drink all the blood spilled as a result of secession, and as such hallucinogenic expectations were proved false, unenthusiastic Confederates reconsidered. Some hoped to sit out the war as neutrals, and the departure of volunteers concentrated dissent among those left behind. Deserters sought out the upland areas where population was thin and apprehension difficult. Furthermore the antebellum political culture there emphasized states' rights, limited government, and low taxes, in the Democratic tradition of Jefferson and Jackson. The Confederate constitution reflected this localism, but the Davis administration in Richmond could hardly fight a states' rights war. It seized railroads, built factories, and dominated the commanding heights of the economy. Many original secessionists were appalled, and as hardships multiplied, disaffection spread.

Ever harsher critiques of the administration proliferated. Governors like Joseph Brown of Georgia assailed President Davis for violating constitutional principles, specifically denouncing conscription. As the casualty count mounted, war-weariness concentrated around such dissenters, some of whom, like Governor Brown himself, became postwar Republicans. One North Carolina politician recalled that almost everywhere "original secessionists lost the favor of the people" early in the war. In the Confederate congressional elections of mid-1863, a loose anti-administration or "Conservative" opposition mostly won, the terminology implying continuity with the sectional moderates of 1860. Conservatives sought negotiations with the Union government, at least as a tactical ploy. President Davis's intransigent refusal left them few options, but Conservatives hoped to maintain their status as good Southerners while somehow nudging the region toward a peace settlement.

Elite criticism resonated differently in the up-country. Ironically the fighting devastated the Upper South first while leaving the secessionist heartland mostly intact. The war took an astonishing toll: 250,000 Southern soldiers died, an incredible one of every four white men of military age. In early 1862 the Confederate government resorted to mass conscription for the first time in

American history. Eventually white men between seventeen and fifty were liable to the army, with men up to sixty subject to militia service. Draft exemption policies were bitterly resented by those who were drafted. The twenty-slave law exempted large slaveholders or overseers; this controversial and much-modified policy prompted complaints of class injustice. Moreover, in the nonplantation counties most of the able-bodied male population went to the front, leaving wives and children behind to provide for themselves—rampant inflation soon reducing army pay to derisory levels. Many of these same upland regions became battlefields, with food stripped either by the Northern invaders or by the Confederates themselves, through the tax-in-kind law or simple seizure. Privation thus riddled the home front, putting pressure on soldiers to come home to feed and protect their families.

A polarization ensued in the up-country. Coerced Confederates sought to ignore the conflict, but the draft made neutrality impossible. Able-bodied men took to the woods, fed by supportive family or neighbors, and the government moved toward harsher measures. There were numerous Confederate atrocities: a mass hanging of Union men in northeast Texas and a collective execution of captured draft evaders in North Carolina. Family members suspected of shielding draft evaders were tortured, and homes were sometimes torched as well. The individual motivations for draft resistance ranged from simple self-interest to localism to class-tinged ideological opposition. Farming became impossible, and draft evaders raided Confederate sympathizers for food. The circumstances created politicized Unionists and armed bands of "Tories" or "Mossbacks," and some 100,000 whites from the Confederacy joined the Union army.

Resisters and Unionists were a minority in all but the poorest mountain areas. Some were sheltered by the community, others were despised by Confederate neighbors. A Northern reporter observed that the Appalachian struggle became "a war of extermination . . . a kind of Vendetta." Upper-class Southerners, those sharing the regional consensus on the war, mostly remained loyal to the Confederacy. Collective trauma and hatred bound most people together. Nearly every family had someone in the army, and as long as General Lee was performing miracles, most Confederates persevered. In the plantation belt, at least off the line of Northern invasion, Confederate citizens probably held out hope until near the end. An open peace candidate, W. W. Holden, did run for governor of North Carolina in mid-1864, but despite widespread popular frustration he was defeated amid charges of treason. Lincoln's resort to emancipation made potential defeat look to the South like annihilation. Only at the end did outright peace sentiment become widespread, and even then "Tories" remained beyond the pale.

The animosity between ex-Confederates and wartime dissidents became a fundamental reality of postwar politics. Unionist alienation yielded native white Republican—or "scalawag"—sentiment. The Unionists' racial views remained retrograde, though most moved toward an emancipationist position as the conflict went on. But race was a secondary issue; these eventual Republicans cut loose from the regional consensus over secession and war. Scholars generally depict scalawag sentiment in class and regional terms, as a movement concentrated in nonslaveholding enclaves in the highlands. As a collective electoral phenomenon this is surely right; only in the poorer upland areas did white Republican votes ever become substantial. Unionists often viewed their persecution in explicit class terms, seeing secession as an undemocratic coup. The "rich man's war, poor man's fight" angle was a mainstay of anti-Confederate rhetoric. Still, Union sentiment subsumed explicit class consciousness. For the dissident minority, traumatized at the hands of the Confederate government and their Rebel neighbors, wartime loyalties overrode everything else.

Union sentiment also crossed class lines, most obviously among those who would rise into Reconstruction leadership. A few slaveholders quietly questioned the morality of slavery, and some wealthy men were embittered by the Davis administration. Before the war Whiggish or Conservative politics often predominated in the richest plantation regions. As the war fulfilled their worst predictions, many planters turned on Southern rights extremists. Mississippi's James Lusk Alcorn wailed: "Our negroes will soon be ashes in our hands, our lands valueless without them. Oh, curse the democratic party for the ruin they have brought me, and give me, Oh God . . . the pleasure of witnessing their tears of lamentation." In northern Alabama, former slaves recalled their masters denouncing Jeff Davis and the secessionists *to them* in private. Moreover Union forces occupied many areas along the Mississippi and other rivers early in the war. Loyalty oaths to the Union could secure planters permission to ship cotton northward when it was extravagantly profitable. But such collaboration opened them to retaliation. Some planters found themselves cooperating with their own slaves against Confederate forces. For some this trajectory would propel them into Reconstruction politics. Planter scalawags were not numerous, but their social position made them important.

Secession and war thus created a diverse constituency of whites who thought of themselves as "Union" men. Many people were Union relative to whatever scale seemed right for their locality and class. But one could be a Union man in the sense of once being an elitist Whig or opposing the Southern rights Democratic candidacy of Breckinridge in 1860. The crucial usage was probably "cooperationism" in the secession winter, but that covered everything from conditional secessionism to outright opposition. Furthermore, across the plantation South most prosperous people acceded to Confederate rule. Networks of elite "Conservatives" escaped the battlefield through connections, occupying civil positions or safe military ones. These nominal Confederates often favored peace, but not to the extent of open treason. Thus Union politics for many consisted, in practice, of mental reservations to be expressed when safe. The experience was far different in upland areas prone to class-drenched disaffection: "Unconditional Unionism" in the sense of an actual preference for Northern victory, even for emancipation. For politicized draft resisters, Unionist refugees, and federal veterans, wartime choices were more relevant than behavior before or during the secession crisis. These Unconditional Unionists often found the compromised "Union" men on the other side during the war, sometimes as draft agents or local militia. One North Carolina leader complained of the "ultra old line War Whigs" and their postwar tendency to stigmatize genuine peace men. These were the poles of Union sentiment, lumped together under a common name, along with every possible position in between. The term "Union" obscured as much as it revealed.

Union politics, of whatever shade, created the white constituency for the Republican party. For decades after the war, whites would call themselves Union far more readily than Republican. Most thought of the issue as the decisive determinant of their politics, and often their lives. All shared opposition to the dominant states' rights Democratic tendency, and a belief that they were entitled to protection and public favor. This made them de facto allies of the victorious Union army and placed them in an uneasy association with an anti-slavery Northern Republican party. If the Union minority sought influence, they needed all the help available, but their position had difficult consequences. White dissidents were few, outside of the highlands, relative to the mass of emancipated slaves. These African-American allies of circumstance were truly alienated from Southern society, seeking the entire overthrow of the racial status quo.

Among slaves, and also the free black minority, the secession crisis aroused tremendous anticipation. Secessionists proclaimed the threat to slavery, and the slaves understood the implications. One black speaker told of "the secret anxiety of the slaves in Florida to know all about President Lincoln's election," reminding listeners of his own prediction of the war. Postwar testimony suggests that slaves monitored the behavior about them, pumping the few white dissidents or eccentrics for information. The slave grapevine spread fact and destabilizing rumor far and wide. But acting upon this knowledge was suicidal, given the heightened vigilance. In Texas, for example, an insurrection scare occurred during the 1860 presidential election campaign, and several slaves were lynched on the basis of unclear evidence. The same thing happened after secession near Huntsville, Alabama. Outside Natchez, slaves began discussing what they might do if the Union army came. Local grandees whipped confessions out of participants, keeping notes of their torture sessions. They killed thirty-odd people, extralegally, for subversive, if unseemly, conversation.

Premature glee among the slaves was not discreet. Still, as masters and overseers left to fight, the balance of power shifted. Officials in central Alabama warned that able-bodied white men were now outnumbered a thousand to one, a wild exaggeration that suggests raw fear. Small wonder that the Confederate Congress repeatedly exempted plantation owners and overseers from the draft. Discipline depended on force, and plantation mistresses, teenaged sons, and elderly relatives could not employ that threat. One escapee derided female-run plantations, confident that he could come and go as he chose. Soldiers could deter outright rebellion, but they could not keep day-to-day discipline. Nor could slaveowners provide the normal material incentives of tobacco, molasses, and sugar. Social control naturally disintegrated as slaves stopped working and awaited events.

Had the Southern cause prevailed, it is unclear in what form slavery could have survived. Former U.S. senator James Hammond, of "cotton is king" notoriety, discovered he could not manage his slaves without his sons or resident overseers. On one of his plantations someone had drilled a hole in his barn, appropriating quantities of food. The slaves watched him sullenly, but he knew "the roar of a single cannon of the Federal's would make them frantic—savage cutthroats & incendiaries." Confederate crop seizures infuriated Hammond, and these complaints were widespread. The army also impressed tens of thousands of slave laborers for fortifications. These workers were overworked, given the urgency of the Yankee threat, often with insufficient food and in unhealthy conditions. They were also exposed to outside information, shown the places where the threat of invasion was more pressing, then sent back home to enlighten their fellow slaves. The process undermined slaveholders' control of their fiefdoms.

As the Union army approached, the situation became still more urgent. Masters relocated thousands of slaves from threatened areas, and it proved difficult to provide for them. Social disruption spread far and wide, even in places like Texas, distant from the front lines. Many slaves, especially young men, took their chances on escape in anticipation of such removals. Some made it through the lines, and a few did more than that, like Harriet Tubman with her service as a spy. Sometimes escaping slaves performed feats that anticipated future political leadership. Robert Smalls gathered family and friends and took a ship out of Charleston Harbor in a bold escape, making himself a national hero. A few years later he would be in Congress.

The safer route was to wait for the federal army to arrive, or await an opportunity to escape with family members. Even before the Emancipation Proclamation, thousands of "contrabands," as General Benjamin Butler termed them, took shelter in

Union camps. With the proclamation, and with the invasion of perhaps half of the Confederacy by war's end, the refugees numbered in the hundreds of thousands. The most overtly disruptive aspect of this situation was the enrollment of blacks as soldiers, which often featured patriotic oratory on egalitarian themes by recruiters. The U.S. Colored Infantry served in segregated units, under white officers, and under discriminatory circumstances in terms of pay and treatment. But in terms of shredding slavery, none of this mattered. Few things could have more thoroughly upended the system than politicized black troops, often led by anti-slavery officers.

Black troops attacked slavery with zeal. In the spring of 1865 a raid on Henry Ravenel's South Carolina plantation was a "Night of horrors!" Soldiers came "to tell the negroes they were free & should no longer work for him. They used very threatening language with oaths & curses." A local escapee guided the troops. When the slaves proved hesitant, the soldiers had little patience: they reportedly threatened to shoot the hands if they were still at work when they returned. The soldiers distributed guns, and soon Ravenel's hands bridled at overseers and gang labor. Despite all this, Ravenel refused to announce freedom for another ten weeks. He first had to persuade himself it was God's will, which itself suggests how protracted the liberation process would be.

By the war's end, slavery had been swept away in the wake of Union armies. Even in the large portion of the Confederacy that escaped occupation, slavery was transformed before freedom arrived. But what would follow? The sudden freeing of four million human beings is something nearly without precedent in human history—nothing on this scale had happened elsewhere in the New World. The experience of the Civil War had created a constituency, black and also white, opposed to the traditional direction of Southern society. Only the victorious North and its army could reshape things in their favor, and how that would play out would be decided in Washington. Ultimately it would be the Northern public and its anti-slavery majority that determined the prospects for a different South.

2

National Politics: Andrew Johnson and the Lost Compromise

THERE ARE A FEW MOMENTS in American history where the effect of chance, of the influence of a single individual, makes a decisive difference. The assassination of Abraham Lincoln and his replacement with his vice president Andrew Johnson is perhaps the most important one. Historians generally view Johnson as the least flexible leader possible at the most sensitive moment in the nation's peacetime history. President Johnson forced a showdown over the fate of the ex-slaves, and he encouraged the ex-Confederate South toward a policy of confrontation. He claimed to be following his predecessor's policies toward the South, and in a technical sense he was, but the differences between the two men are dramatic.

To understand the government Andrew Johnson inherited, one must look at how the war transformed American racial attitudes, most revealingly through an examination of Abraham Lincoln. Although Lincoln long disliked slavery, before the war he shared many of his successor's racial beliefs and disavowed equality as a goal. In his senatorial debates with Stephen Douglas, he observed that "I am not, nor ever have been, in favor of bringing about in any way the social and political equality of the white and black races—that I am not nor ever have been in favor of making voters or jurors of negroes, nor of qualifying them to hold office, nor to intermarry with white people. . . ." Lincoln said much the same thing on other occasions, but he nonetheless saw slavery as unjust to blacks and undemocratic. He viewed restricting slavery as putting it on the road to ultimate extinction; he talked of emancipation and colonization a century hence. This blend of racism and anti-slavery humanitarianism won him a presidential nomination in 1860 and secured him a Republican majority in the electoral college. Although Lincoln abjured any intention of interfering with slavery where it existed, Deep South "fire-eaters" would not wait to see.

With the outbreak of war, Lincoln was buoyed by a surge of Northern patriotism. To maintain bipartisan support, and to mollify the slaveholding border states, he avoided the subject of slavery. But as the conflict continued, political realities changed. The Northern middle-class public, spearheaded by the Protestant churches, embraced an abolition war, as did the Republican majority in the secession-depleted Congress. Furthermore the flood of African-American refugees seeking freedom, and their eagerness to aid the Union war effort, invited action. In January 1863 Lincoln issued his final Emancipation Proclamation, freeing slaves behind Confederate lines. The government began mass recruitment of black soldiers and sailors, 200,000 of them, some 10 percent of Union enlistees. These policies transformed the war's aims.

These changes antagonized the large Democratic minority, and in 1860 Lincoln had received only 55 percent of the vote in the free states. As a prewar Whig, Lincoln favored government promotion of economic growth, and he welcomed the power that the war centralized in Washington. Democrats, however, distrusted expansive government, especially as it took the form of higher taxes, a draft, and incursions on free speech. The public divided over the administration's conduct of the war. Democrats favoring a negotiated peace won a growing following, especially among immigrants and poorer farmers of Southern origins in the lower Ohio valley. These "copperheads" resented the competition that emancipated slaves might bring. In July 1863 the implementation of the draft prompted a major uprising in New York City, with mostly Irish crowds torching an orphanage and lynching perhaps a dozen blacks. More than a hundred residents were killed in this bloodiest urban uprising in American history.

Racism was pervasive in the antebellum North, even among anti-slavery Republicans. Still, as the public polarized, hatred for the slaveholding secessionists and their copperhead allies changed racial attitudes. Liberation became integral to Northern patriotism. After the New York draft riots, patrician businessmen promoted black military recruitment in a nativism-soaked rebuke to the mobs. Everywhere Republican majorities repealed one form of legal discrimination after another. And across the South, Yankee soldiers shouted the "Battle Cry of Freedom" and sang of a biblical Jubilee for slaves. Protestant churches likewise rang with Julia Ward Howe's words: "In the beauty of the lilies Christ was born across the sea / With a glory in His bosom that transfigures you and me / As he died to make men holy, let us die to make men free / While God goes marching on." This reading of the war's meaning resonated with the utopian Puritan origins of New England and the areas it influenced, the upper tier of Northern settlement. Churchgoing Protestants experienced a heady surge of egalitarian idealism. Abolitionists like William Lloyd Garrison and Frederick Douglass went from pariahs to feted prophets of a just cause, welcome even at the White House. During wartime, people often grow to believe their slogans, and for many idealistic Northerners, secession gave racism an unpatriotic aura.

Lincoln increasingly voiced this ideological ferment. At Gettysburg he spoke of a "new birth of freedom," and Jeffersonian phrases like "all men are created equal" took on fresh meaning. But the administration's stiffening line also polarized Northern opinion. Immediately after the preliminary Emancipation Proclamation, Republicans lost scores of seats in Congress. In the presidential election of 1864 the Democratic platform declared the war a failure, and candidate George B. McClellan called for a negotiated reunion with slavery intact. Lincoln refused to retract his emancipation pledge, even as defeat seemed likely, and the consequence was a clear choice at the ballot box. Fortuitously, battlefield successes at Atlanta and elsewhere handed Republicans a resounding victory. Lincoln seized his mandate to push a Thirteenth Amendment to the Constitution, which would end American slavery forever.

By the spring of 1865 Lincoln's speeches sounded different. In his second inaugural address he depicted the conflict as collective punishment for sin, as God's justice even if "every drop of blood drawn with the lash, shall be paid by another drawn with the sword. . . ." In his last public speech Lincoln went further. He publicly stated his preference that in reconstructed Louisiana the vote should be conferred "upon the very intelligent, and on those who serve our cause as soldiers." It may not have been equality, but it was light-years from where he, and the Republican majority, had been only a few years before. While Lincoln apparently decided against mass enfranchisement as a condition of postwar Reconstruction, it seems unlikely that had he lived, he would have remanded the emancipated slaves to the will of their former masters. Still, on the specific issue of the restoration of the Southern states, his successor could point to wartime precedents.

From early in the war, Lincoln began the process of reunion, setting up Unionist state governments in occupied portions of Louisiana, Virginia, Arkansas, and eventually Tennessee. In December 1863 he announced his 10 percent plan, providing that whenever that sliver of the white population pledged future loyalty, he would sanction elections and recognize the results. In practice, Confederate sympathizers would not choose to participate as long as the war continued. Lincoln had no intention of allowing Confederates or even halfhearted Union men to dominate these governments, and he pressed his allies to emancipate the slaves. Nonetheless the Republican majority in Congress became uneasy about the authority the chief executive had assumed and what the postwar governments would look like.

The issue came to a head over Louisiana in the election year of 1864. Louisiana's constitutional convention abolished slavery and called for black access to public education. Still, it refrained from enfranchising African Americans, despite the presence of a substantial number of antebellum free blacks and Afro-Creoles. Radical U.S. congressmen wondered why educated, prosperous, and loyal men should not vote. Republicans, with few dissenting votes, proposed an alternative plan. The Wade-Davis bill stated that when half the number of prewar voters swore future loyalty, elections would be held and constitutions drawn up. This procedure would make for a slower restoration, allowing for greater loyal influence and congressional oversight. The states might then resume representation in Washington, at the discretion of Congress. But only those who could take the "ironclad" oath of past loyalty could vote, which ensured Unionist supremacy for some period after peace returned. While not mandating universal suffrage, the measure opened access to the courts to blacks, and envisioned a more exacting probation than Lincoln's plan. Lincoln pocketvetoed the bill, and when he died the status of the Southern states was still unresolved. In his final speech he referred to his Louisiana creation as provisional. That said, a pattern of executive initiative was well established, and Lincoln's successor could turn the wartime precedents to suit his own Reconstruction policy.

In April 1865 Andrew Johnson was suddenly elevated to the presidency. In some respects his lower-class origins were reminiscent of Lincoln's: Johnson was an orphan, a runaway tailor's apprentice, whose wife taught him to read. His experiences shaped him into a combative leader. Going into politics in nonslaveholder-dominated east Tennessee, he became a strong Democrat in the Jeffersonian/Jacksonian tradition of states' rights, strict construction, and limited government—and in that sense his postwar constitutional views were quite consistent. As a senator he remained something of an outsider in the aristocratic Southern delegation, proclaiming his devotion to the Union.

When the secession crisis came, Johnson defied popular opinion under circumstances of personal bravery. He barely escaped Tennessee, being the sole senator remaining from the seceded states, and he returned as Lincoln's military governor. Johnson strongly backed the Unconditional Unionist faction, and he became a Northern hero, a symbol of Unionist defiance. He called repeatedly for the execution and impoverishment of Rebel traitors. In 1864 Johnson won nomination as vice president on the Union ticket in a bid for bipartisan and regional balance. His inauguration in March 1865 was a disaster, an inebriated rant, but a month later the assassin John Wilkes Booth made him president.

On the racial issues that would dominate Reconstruction, Johnson's views were very different from those of Lincoln or the Republican majority. As military governor in Tennessee he did back administration policy on emancipation, and on one occasion he promised the contrabands he would be their "Moses." Unlike Lincoln, though, the slaveholder Johnson had never showed a distaste for the peculiar institution. He once told black leaders that though he had owned slaves, "I have been their slave instead of their being mine." His private views reflected resentment toward blacks, especially as criticism of his civil rights policies grew. After a meeting with Frederick Douglass and others went badly, he told his private secretary: "Those d——d sons of b——s thought they had me in a trap. I know that d——d Douglass, he's just like any nigger, & he would sooner cut a white man's throat than not." Johnson avoided such venom in public, and indeed he initially kept his own opinions opaque. Still, his inclinations were consistent with his public policies.

President Johnson's racial views and his long-standing Jacksonian Democratic convictions both pushed him toward the same policy. He wanted to restore the ex-Confederate states with as little fuss as possible. He also distrusted the Radical Republicans as lax in their constitutional views and fanatical in their sentimental enthusiasm for the freedpeople. Johnson saw little need for conditions to protect either the freedmen or, more surprisingly, white Unionists, though he doubtless expected they would have influence. In May 1865, dismissing Republican talk of black enfranchisement, he issued his blueprint for North Carolina and soon thereafter for those other Southern states without recognized governments. These proclamations drew on Lincoln's 10 percent plan: the bulk of ex-Confederate soldiers and civilians would take an oath of future loyalty, resume their citizenship under the United States, and then white voters would create new constitutions. If satisfactory, the president would recognize them, and the process of Reconstruction would then hopefully be over. Johnson did bar participation by the former Confederate leadership and those worth more than twenty thousand dollars in property; this provision minimized their role in the various constitutional conventions. The grandees would apply for individual pardons for their crimes, which the president bestowed by the thousands in the months to come.

Congress was not due to reconvene until December 1865, so the president had six full months to get his Presidential Reconstruction governments operating without interference. President Johnson placed implementation of the process in the hands of his appointed provisional governors, who were generally of anti-secession and Conservative backgrounds. The constitutional conventions were told that to win his recognition, they had to repeal the ordinances of secession, ratify the Thirteenth Amendment outlawing slavery, and disavow the Rebel debt. Most ex-Confederates were expecting far more rigorous terms, especially from Andrew Johnson with his wartime talk of hangings and confiscation. Now they could resume state power within weeks of surrender. Their ex-nemesis became popular, and ex-Confederates rushed to reconstruct their states.

Southern whites were relieved to have the killing over and escape with their lives and property. Under the threat of prosecution, those seeking pardons avoided provocative actions. Their pliancy was likely temporary, but under occupation and faced with a united president and Congress, they might have made concessions. Had Lincoln lived, the probability is that Republicans would have insisted on legal protection of basic black freedoms, short of equal suffrage, and might have been able to make it stick. Ex-Confederates likely would have avoided the actions that outraged the North and guaranteed more rigorous terms. Instead President Johnson, in his eagerness to conciliate his late opponents, assured them that they would regain power with minimal concessions; they naturally recalibrated their expectations upward. Presidential support persuaded them that the misgivings of the Republican majority, and Northern sentiment generally, could be disregarded. It was a risky decision.

As the Presidential Reconstruction governments took shape, white Southerners responded to pressing fears of what emancipation meant. Once it appeared that harsh measures were not likely, politicians turned to their next priority, getting the freedmen under control. Opinion leaders understood that slavery was gone, but their understanding of freedom reflected white fears more than black aspirations. Emancipation had been unruly. Thousands of freedpeople were on the roads, looking to reunite family or simply heading elsewhere. Plantation owners urgently

wanted laborers back to work so they could take advantage of
high cotton prices. Their worst nightmare had just become real:
emancipation looked like anarchy, an invitation to theft, vagrancy, and a retrogression to African barbarism. Slavery had
given whites such a strong conviction of racial incapacity that
any alternative view looked mad, like denying gravity. Someone
in authority simply had to monitor the freedpeople's behavior, either the state or employers, and preferably both.

The agenda of repression drew generously on Northern
precedents. During the war, Union officers had dealt with hundreds of thousands of black refugees. People flooded into camps,
and they trailed after the armies on the march. Sometimes the results were benign for the "contrabands," as with General
William T. Sherman's order of January 1865, which envisioned
the confiscation and redistribution of much of the South Carolina and Georgia coasts. Harsher treatment was more common.
Union authorities broadly implemented racially discriminatory
policies, often on military grounds of keeping order. Army commanders wanted to see the contrabands go back to work, if only
on abandoned plantation lands. Authorities repeatedly decreed
labor codes for black plantation laborers, which sanctioned low
wages and rigorous working conditions. After Confederate resistance collapsed, such codes were extended elsewhere. A sort of
tough-love mentality took hold among the Union officers. The
freedmen's supervisor in Louisiana, Thomas Conway, urged:
"Hire them out! Cut wood! Do anything to avoid a state of idle-
ness." Especially in the cities, federal officers initially implemented pass systems targeted at the black unemployed. The
army even shared police tasks with municipal authorities. The
evident intent was to keep as many freedmen as possible working in the countryside.

The culmination of these policies was the Bureau of
Refugees, Freedmen, and Abandoned Lands, popularly known

as the Freedmen's Bureau. Passed by the Republican majority in Congress in March 1865, the Bureau reflected ambivalent Northern attitudes toward African Americans. Led by General O. O. Howard, this military agency had an array of duties. It became the first real federal experiment in social welfare, albeit a temporary one. Many of its functions were uncontroversial, such as the massive food relief provided to white and black refugees. It also cooperated with Northern church and abolition society efforts to found freedmen's schools and send teachers. On the crucial labor issue, the Bureau mitigated the initial rigor of the military policies. Hundreds of local agents provided recourse against physical abuse and employer fraud, aid that was not forthcoming through local governments. But the Bureau's basic policy was to induce planters and freedmen to sign annual labor contracts at a standard rate of wages; the object was to school both planters and their ex-slaves in the ways of free labor while monitoring the outcome. The intent was benign, but agents demonstrated a lively sense of the dangers of vagrancy and the urgent desire to encourage a work ethic. Howard and his Bureau also disabused the freedpeople of the prospect of land redistribution, once Johnson's pardons restored hundreds of thousands of acres to the planter elite.

Southern leaders perceived that the authorities had conceded their right to legislate on freedpeople as a class. As Governor James Throckmorton of Texas observed, "I do believe we will be enabled to adopt a coercive system of labor." The army had discriminated against black refugees readily enough when convenient, and the Northern states had vagrancy laws of their own. A more fundamental problem was the prevalent expectation among both federal officers and Southern planters that freedmen should return to work, instantly, under circumstances that resembled their previous condition. Modern scholars have been justly critical of the repressive racial implications of these policies, but they have underemphasized their sheer impracticality. Freedpeople were so disoriented by the transformation of their lives that many were likely incapable of productive labor. Realistically, some lapse of time might have been expected for them to reorient themselves. Indifferent labor did not herald permanent dependency; as it happened, most freedmen went back to work soon enough. More generous provision of temporary federal food relief might have eased the transition away from slavery, counteracting planters' coercive inclinations. The imperative emphasis on contracts instead encouraged the planters to enact the vagrancy legislation they thought necessary.

The Black Codes took shape in the 1865 constitutional conventions and subsequent state legislatures. In some generally unnoticed respects, the codes extended important freedoms to emancipated slaves. The right to sue and be sued, to sign contracts, to own property, to marry legally—these all had important implications. However circumscribed by discrimination, it was difficult to prevent freedpeople from using the legal system to express their grievances. For example, a study of postwar law around Vicksburg found that even under Mississippi's severe Black Codes, freedpeople prosecuted cases of fraud and violence. Publicity and inconvenience might have some deterrent effect, even if actual redress was rare. It proved hard to make the courts as repressive as the lash. Whites perceived a frightening loss of racial control, which encouraged the wave of extralegal violence throughout the period.

Legislators did their best to relieve their constituents' fears by making freedpeople a subordinate class. The specifics vary from state to state, but the general intent was unmistakable. Lawmakers severely punished interracial marriage, though not interracial sex, which would have been inconvenient. Texas inaugurated the convict lease and decreed racial segregation on railroads. Apprenticeship laws were particularly reminiscent of slavery: orphans in North Carolina were to labor for former masters, explicitly, in preference to grandparents or other relatives. In various states, blacks had to pay a regressive poll (or head) tax, with the proceeds devoted to the whites-only school system. Freedpeople were generally banned from ownership of firearms. It even proved difficult to repeal the antebellum prohibitions on blacks testifying against whites, a pressing matter in view of plantation owners' tendency toward physical chastisement.

Lawmakers' overriding concern was plantation discipline, and Mississippi's Black Codes illustrated these priorities. Vagrancy statutes spelled out that blacks were to sign an annual labor contract by the second Monday in January, unless exempted by local authorities. Violators were liable to arrest and being rented out as laborers to pay the fines. Outside city limits, freedpeople were banned from rental (though not purchase) of land. These measures bolstered the bargaining position of landowners and forced freedmen and freedwomen back to work as plantation hands. Lawmakers exhausted their imagination in repressive legislation. One Mississippi statute decreed that blacks committing "riots, routs, affrays, trespasses, malicious mischief, cruel treatment to animals, seditious speeches . . . or committing any other misdemeanor, the punishment of which is not specifically provided for by law," would receive a fine of up to one hundred dollars and up to thirty days' imprisonment. The final quoted clause was emblematic: the law allowed authorities to penalize nearly anything. This made sense, for freedpeople could challenge their accustomed place in a thousand subtle ways, and lawmakers sought to repress them all.

These exacting laws reflected urgent fears; perhaps as things settled, their rigor might have been modified. Still, they looked permanent, and the Black Codes became a lightning rod for Northern criticism. The Presidential Reconstruction governments raised other concerns, their composition perhaps the leading one. Secessionist Democrats were unpopular and often unpardoned at the moment, so voters turned to perceived moderates at the constitutional conventions. Even so, most of the leaders elected under Presidential Reconstruction had been complicit in the Confederate war effort, except in Tennessee where the Unconditional Unionist government—established by then military governor Andrew Johnson—had disfranchised Rebels. Under Governor William G. Brownlow, developments here little resembled what was happening elsewhere, or rather resembled them in reverse. Tennessee figured as a Radical horror story for the rest of the white South, which highlighted the point that in ten of the eleven states in rebellion, ex-Confederates soon regained state power. This left ex-slaves and the Unconditional Unionist minority exposed to retaliation within months of Northern victory.

Thus as the fall of 1865 gave way to winter, President Johnson surveyed the fruits of his policy with unease. While most constitutional conventions had complied with his stated conditions, several had needed arm-twisting. Some had refused to ratify the Thirteenth Amendment or attached conditions interpreting it narrowly. Also, in the Deep South ex-secessionists frequently won office under the new governments, and Johnson found himself pardoning ex-Confederate leaders so they could take office. This was not exactly the politic show of penitence he was hoping for, and Johnson privately expressed dismay. He was aware of Northern reservations, and on one occasion he actually suggested that giving a few blacks the vote would disarm Radical criticism. But faced with the alternative of disavowing his handiwork, not to mention newfound Southern admirers, he soldiered on. One after another he recognized the Southern governments and proclaimed them satisfactory.

When Congress gathered in December, the Republican majority was less impressed. A host of ex-Confederate dignitaries now presented themselves for readmission, including ten Rebel generals, six cabinet officers, and nine congressmen. Confederate vice president Alexander Stephens was elected to the Senate, and the bulk of his comrades could not have taken an oath of wartime loyalty. Overlooked in the Northern criticism was the fact that most of these officials had resisted secession, at least for a while, and that many had followed Stephens in seeking a negotiated peace. One could also argue that electing ex-Confederates indicated acceptance of the results of the war, and who better to lead the region in reunion than the established leadership? But until safely back in the Union, the Southern states were on probation before the Northern electorate, and President Johnson's sanction encouraged them to disregard the probable consequences.

The Northern public recoiled, and Republican congressmen had ample cause for alarm. All possibility of further guarantees would have evaporated were Southern Congressmen admitted, and the Black Codes would stand as law. Furthermore their presence raised the possibility of ex-Confederates joining their Northern copperhead allies and taking over the government; the end of the three-fifths constitutional ratio in counting slaves meant the South would receive still more representatives. These were dire prospects so soon after the rebellion, easily averted by excluding all eighty Southern claimants. The Constitution provides that the House and Senate determine their own membership, and wartime loyalty oaths already barred most of the Southern representatives. Almost all Republicans agreed the delegations must not be readmitted for the time being. There was an issue of constitutional principle; Johnson claimed the strict-construction high ground, but Republicans doubted that the executive could restore eleven rebellious states unilaterally, without legislative assent. For the next year and more, President Johnson recognized the ex-Confederate states as being in the Union while

Congress maintained that they were not—until further conditions were met. Around this anomalous situation, a constitutional meltdown would ensue.

Few initially thought an impasse likely. Radical Republicans like Thaddeus Stevens, of course, rejected the president's "insane course." But Andrew Johnson was popular in late 1865, and the rejectionist position was initially limited to racial egalitarians. Southern whites frequently termed all Republicans "Radicals," a rhetorical device that reflected their lack of acuity about Northern opinion. At this moment the imprecise nomenclature was particularly misleading, because there was a wide array of Republican views and preferences. Moderates generally represented closely contested districts, and they often reflected the party's pragmatic, business-oriented constituency. These leaders distrusted their more Radical colleagues—Senator Charles Sumner in particular—as self-righteous ideologues. The moderate Republicans did not seek a constitutional crisis; they sought to fine-tune Presidential Reconstruction, not overturn it entirely. They assumed Johnson shared their concern for the political future of the party that elected him. Thus in early 1866 a parade of respected moderates trooped in to see the president. They emerged well pleased, because whether from tactic or from some personal quirk the president tended not to disagree with visitors. The dignitaries thought they had achieved a meeting of the minds. Johnson more accurately concluded that his constitutional views and policy preferences were diametrically opposed.

The influential Senator Lyman Trumbull of Illinois proposed two bills that encapsulated the moderate Republican approach. The first was an extension of the Freedmen's Bureau, which would allow the ex-slaves access to a nondiscriminatory legal structure. The need seemed evident, and the humanitarian agency enjoyed wide support in the North. The other legislation established the meaning of liberation. Most Northerners retained strong racial prejudices, and Republican proposals to enfranchise blacks in Northern states fared badly before the electorate, but Northerners mostly understood emancipation as conveying certain rights. Thus Trumbull's civil rights proposal outlawed the Black Codes. It prevented states from infringing equality before the law, short of suffrage, and provided redress in federal courts. The bill broadly anticipated what would become the Fourteenth Amendment, and Republicans coalesced behind it as simple justice.

Congress passed both the Freedmen's Bureau and then the civil rights bills by large margins, and to the surprise of nearly all observers, the president vetoed both. Moderate leaders felt personally betrayed. A president elected with Republican votes suddenly looked like an enemy, controlling the patronage jobs of more than fifty thousand federal officeholders. The veto messages stressed the unprecedented nature of the legislation, establishing safeguards for freedpeople "which go infinitely beyond any that the General Government has ever provided for the white race." The vetoes emphasized the difference as one of constitutional philosophy, and they suggested compromise might still be possible. That possibility soon evaporated, for Johnson highlighted the breach in neon. Responding to a boisterous crowd on Washington's birthday, the president compared his current struggle to restore the Union to the recent rebellion. He responded eagerly when asked to name the traitors of the North: "I say Thaddeus Stevens of Pennsylvania—I say Charles Sumner—I say Wendell Phillips, and others of the same stripe. . . ." The audience applauded uproariously, but the Northern public saw the exchange quite differently.

By the spring of 1866 the political situation resolved itself into the Republican majority's struggle to pass both bills over Johnson's vetoes. The civil rights bill and, eventually, a Bureau renewal passed, which provided an uncommonly clear choice in the fall's congressional election. It was President Johnson and his Reconstruction policy, up or down. Except for the Unionist minority, which moved toward Congress, white Southerners were energized by Johnson's resolute position. Honor was important in the South, and ex-Confederates were becoming restive under their prolonged probation. All the Yankee officers, Bureau agents, and Northern schoolteachers were unsettling their freedmen, and impatient whites wanted them gone. Admiration for Johnson's defiant stand lured white Southerners onto the firing line of one more lost cause. In their enthusiasm they disregarded the destabilizing consequences of a veto-proof Republican majority. They were singularly ill-situated to influence, or even to gauge, Northern opinion. One Washington adviser warned that "the South has got to fill second place all the time, until she has set herself in harmony with the great mass of the people who put down the rebellion." Instead Johnson and his Southern admirers embraced each other as mutual hostages. The South bet on Johnson's political skill, and the president in turn relied on white Southerners' discreet behavior.

Neither was much in evidence. It proved difficult to keep whites from seeking confrontation. Politicians counseled one another to avoid open criticism of Southern behavior, and the attempted cover-up made it difficult to urge restraint. When faced with negative national coverage, North Carolina's Governor Jonathan Worth assailed one "lying villain" responsible, future Republican Albion Tourgée, who sought "to make the North hate us." He warned Tourgée's allies, especially local Quakers, that backing him risked community retaliation. Rather than address the issue of spreading violence, the obviously infuriated governor orchestrated editorial denials in detail. He also spread dubious personal counterattacks on the Northerner's character.

The reports coming from the South were difficult to finesse. The cities became the flashpoint, swollen with wartime refugees and concentrations of poor immigrants. In-migration of African Americans always generated harsh official responses, and in Norfolk and Charleston that spring there were race riots. In early May Memphis suffered a murderous spree. The responsibility for initiating conflict there is unclear, but the results were distressingly concrete. The black proportion of the population more than doubled during the war, and confrontations escalated between white police and black soldiers over control of public space. After the troops were mustered out, there was a street fight over an arrest. White mobs swept into south Memphis, killing scores—forty-five by one count. Several black women testified they had been raped. Not one white would be punished by the authorities, the normal pattern in postwar riots.

Another outbreak in New Orleans had complicated political origins. Under Presidential Reconstruction, Louisiana's ex-Rebels swept into office. In response, some of the Unionist leaders concocted a scheme to reconvene the 1864 constitutional convention and enfranchise the black population, or at least prompt congressional action. The proposal was of questionable legality, and it was provocative to claim legislative authority, but what followed overshadowed everything else. Before the convention gathered on July 30, city officials threatened wholesale arrests, and the delegates met without military protection. In the streets, suffrage supporters confronted white protesters whipped up by the press and backed by the police. Partisans began pelting one another with bricks, and the whites prevailed and began beating black bystanders. The aggravated mob and police then stormed the convention building. Some who fled were beaten to death; one convention attendee, a minister, was shot to death with a white flag in his hands. By the army's reckoning, 37 Republicans were killed, preponderantly freedmen, with another 150 injured. Perhaps one white was killed in the attacking crowd, with another ten injured.

Andrew Johnson blamed the delegates, calling them essentially traitors, adding that the disturbance was "substantially planned" by his congressional opponents. These statements antagonized the electorate, and the riots made it difficult to depict his policies as a success. In addition, Johnson's own conduct frightened people. He referred to the U.S. Congress as illegitimate, inspiring rumors that he might disperse it by force—and apparently he was pondering the idea. An unprecedented crisis could have resulted had the 1866 election results allowed him to claim a majority with the Southern claimants. At one point the president solicited General Ulysses S. Grant's intentions if that were to occur. The shocked Grant responded that "the army will support the Congress as it now is and disperse the other." Grant privately warned subordinates to be prepared to crush any renewed Southern rebellion. Historians have often been critical of the later impeachment of the president, but Johnson's behavior at this time provides often overlooked justification.

Banana-republic maneuvers remained mostly secret, but what was known was unsettling enough. Johnson's followers convened a National Union convention, staking out the middle ground and featuring intersectional amity, but the New Orleans riot's timing undercut the effect. Johnson also fired many hundreds of Republican federal officeholders. Late that summer he addressed the Northern public on his "swing round the circle" tour. This unaccustomed initiative proved a disaster as newspapers reported him giving the same speech over and over. On the platform he seemingly compared his woes to those of Christ crucified, and he spoke of hanging Thaddeus Stevens and other Radicals. Republicans seeded the crowds with hecklers, and Johnson let himself be drawn into undignified exchanges. General Grant, who initially accompanied the president, wrote his wife of the "National disgrace." Even Johnson's closest supporters lapsed into sullen silence.

The Republicans, by contrast, demonstrated electoral savvy, keeping their more vulnerable flanks well hidden. They left black suffrage expediently out of their platform, to the discomfort of Radical Republicans and Deep South Unionists. The Republicans' core proposal was the pending Fourteenth Amendment, which had been passed by Congress and awaited ratification by the states. In response to Johnson's strict-construction viewpoint, Republicans envisioned a Constitution broad enough to protect basic liberties. The amendment basically declared blacks citizens, though not voters. The crucial section provided, "No State shall make or enforce any law which shall abridge the privileges or immunities of citizens of the United States; nor shall any State deprive any person of life, liberty or property, without due process of law; nor deny to any person within its jurisdiction the equal protection of the laws." The legislative intent has been much debated, but in a sense Johnson was right: the amendment revolutionized the Constitution, making an expanded federal government the ultimate protector of civil rights. Other provisions deprived those who had taken an oath of office, and then participated in the rebellion, of the right to hold government positions. Finally, the states would have their congressional representation reduced for the number of males disfranchised. Moderate Republican lawmakers thus presented a palatable alternative to Presidential Reconstruction. If the ex-Confederate states accepted these terms, well and good, but no one knew what would happen if the Southern states prevented ratification.

Whatever the uncertainties the future held, it didn't much matter. Republicans made Andrew Johnson the issue, and the Northern public had seen enough. With the South still unrepresented, Republicans elected 143 congressmen to 48 for administration supporters. Save for the Democratic strength in the border states, Republicans swept everything before them. The outcome was equally substantial in the Senate. It was an emphatic repudiation of a sitting president. Johnson's opponents had far more than the two-thirds majority they needed to pass legislation over his veto, or, if need be, to impeach him. Congress now claimed the popular mandate to prescribe whatever final terms as they saw fit.

For white Southerners, the aftermath of the 1866 election was the moment of truth, the last of a string of fateful choices. Johnson's defeat left them exposed to the will of Congress, unmediated. The gun was cocked, and there was but one alternative to escape unprecedented consequences. If they ratified the Fourteenth Amendment, the process of Reconstruction would probably soon be over. Radical Republicans resisted the notion, hoping for further measures to transform the disloyal region, but most moderates abjured further conditions. When Brownlow's Unionist government in Tennessee ratified the amendment in mid-1866, the state's congressmen were immediately readmitted. If the other Southern states refused to ratify, they were essentially defying the Republican majority to do their worst, and leaving them little alternative. As congressional leader James G. Blaine recalled, "The Southern whites knowingly and willfully brought it upon themselves. The Reconstruction Act would never have been demanded had the Southern States accepted the Fourteenth Amendment in good faith."

For Southern leaders the idea of black suffrage seemed so outlandish that they believed the Northern electorate would reconsider. In the long run they were dead right; the Northerners remained racially prejudiced, and few had positive enthusiasm for illiterate freedmen voting. Northerners would eventually tire of the endless struggle to protect civil rights. But in the meantime Southern leaders sentenced their region to a tumultuous decade of governmental instability and violence. Given how foreseeable the negative consequences were, one is tempted to ask, Why? Beyond barring from office the old ruling class and reducing the South's—currently nonexistent—representation in Congress, it is difficult to see ratification's practical harm, at least relative to the daunting alternative. The Fourteenth Amendment became law anyway, and acceding to Congress's terms would have meant that Southern whites retained control. Only Southern intransigence could have forced Congress to accept black suffrage, and once more defiance of the Yankees was in play.

Perhaps elite self-interest and pride were the crucial motivation: politicians refused to bar themselves even temporarily from office. Decades later, Southern congressman Hilary Herbert thought this provision was the crucial factor in the rejection of the amendment. Still, some leaders warned of danger. In Alabama, Governor Robert M. Patton endorsed ratification, but the president telegraphed his plea to stand firm. The legislature then crushed the amendment, and so Andrew Johnson bestowed one last political benediction on his Southern allies. All the remaining ex-Confederate states turned the measure down decisively, so that the amendment clearly could never be ratified as things stood. The Republican majority was surprised, having simply assumed that their electoral victory would force compliance. By early 1867 it was clear that Congress had either to do something drastic or concede Johnson his way. This latter truly was political suicide, so Republicans steeled themselves for unprecedented legislation.

As Congress pondered Reconstruction, the South's excluded voices made themselves heard. The amendment's rejection changed their political circumstances overnight. The South's ruling class stood on the brink, and one shove might topple it and bring a whole new leadership. Presidential Reconstruction had operated on the assumption that the alienation of Unconditional Unionists could be safely disregarded, but suddenly things looked different. Loyalist leaders from the ex-Confederate states had been demanding black suffrage since the fall, and now a cohort descended on Washington. Tennessee's Unionist government granted African-American suffrage by state law in February. As these events transpired, the most politically aware segments of the black population mobilized in tandem. Evanescent newspapers and organizations appeared, strongly Republican in tone. Across the urban South, marches, meetings, and conventions redoubled pleas for legal equality. African-American and Unionist demands for equal suffrage converged, suggesting that Congress protect both at one blow.

Republicans moved quickly, before the outgoing Thirty-ninth Congress adjourned. If Congress meant to overturn Johnson's governments, the reality was that only some version of universal suffrage could yield loyal majorities, unless they meant to disfranchise masses of ex-Confederates. Black suffrage seemed more democratic than that alternative. As Thaddeus Stevens observed, "The white Union men are in a great minority in each of those states. With them the blacks would act in a body; and it is believed that . . . the two united would form a majority, control the States, and protect themselves." But black suffrage, even limited to the South, was not popular in the North. It needed to happen quickly, while the recent mandate was fresh and the next election far away. Thus Congressional Reconstruction was a hurried affair, enacted in a startlingly offhand fashion for such momentous legislation.

The first Military Reconstruction act, re-passed the very day of Johnson's veto on March 2, was a composite of several proposals, and lawmakers had only vague notions of how it would work. The initial legislation had no implementation mechanism, on the odd assumption that the Southern legislatures would commence the process. In all, four Reconstruction acts were needed to fine-tune the intent of Congress. Moderate Republicans like Senator John Sherman of Ohio were the key players, insisting that the process be finite and that the carrot of readmission be evident. The existing governments were superseded by military authority, though civil officeholders remained in place. The army would oversee registration of a new electorate, which would include the African-American population and exclude those proscribed from office by the proposed Fourteenth Amendment. Elections would then be called to authorize new conventions and elect delegates, and if Reconstruction received a majority, and half the registered electorate voted, the delegates would draft a state constitution. If approved in an election in which at least half the potential electorate took part, it would be forwarded to Congress. The numerical provisions in the second Reconstruction act were baffling: it could require as little as one-quarter of the registered voters to authorize a new constitution, if votes were perfectly distributed, but in practice it required substantially more than half. If successful, and once Congress approved and the state ratified the Fourteenth Amendment, the Reconstruction process concluded. Military oversight then ended, and the state was restored to the Union.

Radical Republicans supported black suffrage, but they were leery of the provisions for a swift and clearly delineated process of restoration. W. W. Holden recalled Thaddeus Stevens telling him that "it would be best for the South to remain ten years longer under military rule, and that during this time we would have Territorial Governors, with Territorial Legislatures, and the government at Washington would pay our general expenses as territories. . . ." Given how things turned out, this approach had retrospective advantages: it would have furthered a military role in repressing terrorism and provided a check on the sort of taxation and subsidy legislation that would do Republicans such political damage. Universal suffrage was an experiment under untried leadership, and some practical experience might not have been amiss. Here, as elsewhere, the demands of short-term political reality as defined by the Northern public prevailed. They wanted swift restoration. Congressman Blaine was certain that a territorial scheme would have meant electoral disaster—"utter overthrow at the initial point of reconstruction policy."

Another congressman reportedly advised that restoration was needed quickly. Then the Southern states could "all be counted on in the presidential election; and, under a favorable administration, whatever further changes are necessary can be easily effected." Moderates also hoped that explicit, final conditions would win substantial white participation.

Still, all Republicans united behind the Reconstruction legislation, and most were hopeful. Johnson's intense unpopularity had enabled them to reshape national politics at one blow, potentially breaking the Democratic regional stranglehold. With military protection and federal government support, the black minority in the reconstructed states might unite with beleaguered Unionists and the few Northern newcomers. With the support of Congress and the military, they might win power through the democratic process, guaranteeing the results of the war once and for all.

Thus the mass of African Americans in the United States received the ballot, changing the national agenda forever. Just as emancipation is difficult to imagine under any circumstances other than secession, universal male suffrage could hardly have come so quickly without Presidential Reconstruction. Had Lincoln lived, it is difficult to see how Northern politics could have polarized so decisively in favor of civil rights; in a way, modern America is indebted to Andrew Johnson's blundering extremism—and Southern intransigence—for the emergence of legal equality as a serious issue. But Johnson would have his revenge: as freedmen entered the political process under Yankee auspices, their enfranchisement would be bitterly resented by the mass of Southern whites. Thus an enormous weight of responsibility fell on the proponents of Reconstruction, and its Northern Republican architects, to make the new order function in spite of infuriated resistance.

3

Emancipation and Terror in the Plantation South

EXTRAORDINARY POLITICAL CONVULSIONS culminated in black suffrage in the former Confederate states, but the social transformation under way was equally dramatic. Four million people, a third of the Southern population, became suddenly free, and no road map existed for such a transition. The distinctive thing about emancipation in the United States, as Eric Foner has argued, is that legal equality came to ex-slaves soon after liberation. Reconstruction therefore was simultaneously a political and labor struggle. For years it was unclear in what form, if any, the plantation system would survive. For large landowners, controlling labor was the crucial issue, along with maintaining social authority. For the emancipated slaves, the urgent question was how free freedom was going to be. The traumatic memory of slavery took precedence, reasserting itself insistently once immediate necessities were met.

How emancipation unfolded made a difference. In much of the Upper South, occupation or invasion destroyed slavery well before the war ended. Chaotic conditions forced experimentation with paying wages, in a de facto progression toward free labor. The situation was different in the half or so of the Confederacy that had escaped prolonged exposure to the federal army.

Texas and much of western Louisiana, for example, nearly went untouched, as did southwest Georgia and central Alabama until the war's final days. In isolated areas the news of Confederate defeat had an unreal quality. Even after Lee's surrender on April 9, 1865, slaveholders within the collapsing Confederacy refused to believe the end had come. Rumors circulated of foreign war, and some fantasized about a Supreme Court decision restoring their slave property. Their situation seemed so awful that realism had few charms.

Even after most of the Confederate commands had surrendered by early May, plantation owners in isolated areas continued to work their restive hands, hoping to get one more crop in the ground. In late May a Georgia master told his slaves that they would probably be freed, but it apparently took a direct order before he started paying them in July. Masters seldom freed anyone until occupation forces arrived. David Harris of Spartanburg, South Carolina, noted Confederate surrender in late April, but things continued much as before. In early June he observed that federal forces had proclaimed emancipation, but when a hand left, he still hoped the Yankees "would give him a good whipping & hasten him back." It was only in mid-August that neighbors freed slaves, in the face of army orders that "we are to pay them, & not drive them off nor correct [whip] them." Having finished most of a crop, Harris finally ordered them away, some four months after Appomattox.

The freedpeople-in-waiting grew exasperated, but they also realized that challenge risked a violent response. Long training as slaves made most leery of direct confrontation. To enjoy their freedom in peace meant having their late masters acknowledge it. Besides, for weeks the roads were swarming with demoralized Confederate veterans; even the planters feared them, and there are ugly reports of racial violence. Union soldiers in Montgomery were horrified to find freedwomen entering camp with their ears hacked off. Full liberation thus awaited the establishment of Yankee garrisons scattered throughout the war's backwaters. In distant Texas, for example, the official announcement had to wait until June 19, the proverbial "Juneteenth." The army routinely dispatched agents into the countryside to announce the official news.

But what would black freedom be like? No one knew, but the ex-masters had some notion of what they preferred. They wanted as much of their accustomed way of life as possible. Few Southern whites questioned the basic values of slavery. Secession would have made no sense if they didn't believe in racial supremacy. They saw the consequences of emancipation as catastrophic—to themselves, certainly, but more broadly to civilized life. North Carolina's Jonathan Worth predicted, "The South is never again—at least for several generations—to be the happy and prosperous country it once was. We who were born here, will never get along with the free negroes. . . . As an inferior race they will degenerate and retard all prosperity." Dominant sentiment viewed blacks as lazy and irresponsible; morally upright planters prided themselves on their accommodation to these unfortunate racial traits. They could not imagine a future in which somebody white wasn't responsible for black behavior.

The crucial issue was plantation management. Before the war, cotton plantations were farmed in a more or less standard fashion. The day was long, "from can't [see] to can't," as the slaves put it, so that even with hours off for meals, hands in the hot summer would put in an exhausting day. Masters didn't expect much enthusiasm, but they did exact a five-and-a-half-day week toiling under someone's watchful eye. Men, women, and older children worked in gangs, under the control of white overseers and black slave drivers. Supervisors generally brandished whips and used them to a varying extent; the threat was always there, and major infractions were punished forcibly. Masters discouraged hands from wandering, with the hated slave patrols whipping those caught off the plantation without written permission. Hands lived together in the slave quarters, except perhaps for a few domestics at the Big House. Once a week, on Saturday nights, slave families received their allotment of food, and those who ran short were out of luck, which encouraged the pilfering that planters complained about endlessly.

The pattern was broadly similar in tobacco and other crops, though there were variations. Louisiana's sugar, for example, required a heavy capital investment for equipment. Large plantations and extreme labor demands characterized the crop, with work often extending round the clock when the cane had to be processed quickly. Perhaps the most distinctive area was along the coasts and sea islands of South Carolina and Georgia, the "Gullah district," where rice and a special form of luxury long-staple cotton were grown. Here, in the unhealthy lowlands, with few whites in yearlong residence, a system developed of each slave having an individual daily task. Once a supervisor inspected the work, the slave was finished. Unhealthy as working in this area tended to be—one study calculated that 66 percent of children born on Georgia rice plantations died by age sixteen— slaves often preferred the task system for the increased leisure and an opportunity to make money in off-hours.

Whatever the crop, owners knew how to farm it in one particular fashion. Planters understood freedpeople would be paid, preferably with a portion of the crop withheld till year's end. Otherwise planters wanted as much of the old system as circumstances would allow. They wanted controls on the laborer's mobility in order to monitor disruptive outside influences. Planters wanted men, women, and children to work, just as they had in the past. They wanted the accustomed hours, and they mostly wanted gang labor under close supervision. And, based on everything they believed, they inclined toward force. A Virginia

planter complained, "the edict has gone forth, that under no circumstances are they to be flogged—hence they are utterly lazy
and negligent." Ex-slaveholders gave up the whip only grudg-
ingly, scarcely believing they could farm along these lines without it.

The freedpeople had preferences too. Especially in the areas
recently freed from Confederate control, euphoric celebration often took precedence. One ex-slave recalled: "Everybody went
wild. We felt like heroes, and nobody had made us that way but
ourselves. We was free. Just like that, we was free." For many,
the first goal was simply to demonstrate they were really at liberty. There was some lingering fear of reenslavement, and departure might foreclose that possibility. Even if they later
returned, as many did, they proved a point. In the summer and
fall of 1865 the roads were laden with migrants, and there were
more emotionally pressing motives than simply testing freedom.
For generations, slavery had scattered families. Teenage children
were routinely sold westward, leaving parents and siblings behind. Husbands and wives were separated, with quantitative evidence suggesting it happened often. The war only intensified
this problem, for thousands of slaves were relocated to Texas and
other interior areas. For masses of liberated people the first order
of business was to return home and find lost loves, parents,
children—if the trail had not gone cold. For decades one saw
newspaper advertisements seeking relatives. John De Forest, a
Freedmen's Bureau official in South Carolina, was not given to
sentiment, but even he understood: "They had a passion, not so
much for wandering, as for getting together; and every mother's
son among them seemed to be in search of his mother; every
mother in search of her children."

Adapting family needs to the legal standards of freedom
raised sensitive issues, especially in terms of perception by Northern observers, a matter of some urgency given how badly the

freedmen needed allies. Slave marriages had no legal sanction, which technically made all children illegitimate. Here, as in much else, the African-American population sought to erase the stigma of slavery. Army authorities were eager to oblige, and chaplains conducted hundreds of thousands of impromptu marriages. The historian Charles Dew located an instance in Virginia of an elderly slave registering his marriage ceremony, but the Bureau ledger indicates that his longtime wife had died some seven years earlier. This arresting posthumous marriage suggests the damage slavery wrought on people's lives.

Not everyone felt this way. Although marriages among former slave couples were legion, thousands more chose not to solemnize their relationships formally. The institution of slave marriage, lacking legal sanction, was more elastic than contemporary Victorian norms. Recent studies suggest that people in the slave quarters distinguished casual cohabitation from committed relationships. For some freedpeople, in some circumstances, the former condition was preferred. Moreover some scholars have argued that under slavery women could leave unsatisfactory relationships with little ill effect, because they were not financially dependent. If they lacked the protection and support that white women could normally expect, they were also spared the expectation of passivity and subordination to men. Thus in making the transition to legal freedom, rather than simply mimicking Victorian norms the freedpeople selectively appropriated what they chose. For example, formal divorces remained rare. To the frustration of sympathetic Bureau agents, the freedpeople tended to dismiss such niceties as expensive technicalities.

The tension between familiar habits and the appeal of a dramatic break was evident in agricultural work. After emancipation many observers described freedwomen as abandoning field labor, though poverty prevented an entire withdrawal. Many freedmen encouraged this transition, relishing the opportunity to support their families and to shield wives and daughters from the unwelcome attentions of supervisors. The appeal of mainstream notions of manhood seems evident, but there is also the issue of female agency. The Bureau's John De Forest decried the "evil of female loaferism," his word choice suggesting that he thought women responsible. In a wider society dominated by notions of "separate spheres," it appears that freedwomen sought the status that Victorian norms afforded them—and to escape from the perceived degradation of field labor. Time at home would contribute to family comfort while garden products would provide some cash as well, independent of the landlord's control. But these changes also imposed a degree of dependency upon husbands that the Reconstruction-era changes in family law intensified. The rejection of slavery meant that black women increasingly achieved the same subordinate status that white women enjoyed, but without the same economic benefits. The Reconstruction of gender expectations was among the most complicated issues brought by emancipation.

In other areas the route toward liberation was more obvious, especially with respect to education. Illiterates had limited job options, and they were ill-situated to negotiate contracts or puzzle out accounts. The practical motivation was real, but the symbolic appeal was potent too: literacy pointed toward equality and citizenship. A spontaneous wave of schooling swept the black community. These efforts meshed well with the priorities of the Northern public, thoroughly sold on the benefits of public education. Local initiatives could thus count on substantial material aid. The Freedmen's Bureau subsidized school construction, and led by the "Christian General" O. O. Howard it cooperated with Protestant groups. The anti-slavery American Missionary Association established hundreds of schools in larger towns where military protection existed. Northern Methodists, Congregationalists, and other denominations sent teachers southward, totaling

perhaps five thousand "Yankee schoolmarms" in all. Higher education blossomed too, and America's major black colleges
mostly were founded during this era.

The zeal for education was all-pervasive, but religion was
equally important and more revealing of future tensions. The
freedpeople struggled to define their desires in the face of hostile
Southern whites while maintaining some autonomy from their
Northern allies. Before the Civil War, blacks held subordinate
status in the white congregations, primarily in the regionally
dominant Southern Methodist and Southern Baptist churches.
These denominations had split from their national churches over
slavery, and they promoted a pronounced Southern viewpoint.
After emancipation most freedpeople fled them, and a free-
for-all for their loyalties ensued. For example, two African
Methodist denominations (the AME and AME Zion) were challenged by the national Methodist Episcopal Church, well sup-
plied with missionaries and the prestige of the victorious North.
The Northern Methodists welcomed the ex-slaves and white
Unionists into one Radical church purged of caste distinctions
and blessed with monetary resources. But the national church
could be infuriatingly obtuse: one Methodist bishop hoped to
preserve the freedpeople from "the superstitions of witchcraft
and of demons; and to prevent them from degenerating into wild
fanaticism." The spiritual/ideological challenge for freedpeople
was whether race-specific institutions were appropriate, or even
justified, now that slavery was gone. What would Radical Republican religion be? Northern Republicans and their black political allies often drew different conclusions.

All the new freedoms, practical and symbolic, came together
over plantation labor, the fundamental site of social struggle.
Once immediate euphoria passed, many freedpeople returned
home. Jobs were scarce in the region's few cities, and only a
handful headed north, so farm labor was the inevitable choice.

For African-American lives to improve in tangible ways, gang labor and other hated practices had to change. But the Black Codes and contracts demonstrated landowners' contrary preferences. The freedmen found ways of expressing their displeasure. In late 1865 rumors spread that the federal government would issue them "forty acres and a mule." General Sherman's confiscation order and, briefly, Bureau policy had suggested the possibility. The notion that free blacks would labor for their ex-masters seemed counterintuitive. As one elderly freedman put it, "What's de use of being free if you don't own enough land to be buried in? Might juss as well stay slave all yo' days." Freedmen often perceived the land as theirs by right, and as Christmas approached, expectations of conflict grew. The Freedmen's Bureau took the threat seriously enough to emphasize that any outbreak would be repressed. Planters spoke of a coming insurrection, in real or feigned alarm, and it served as an excuse for vagrancy legislation. If there was ever any threat of an actual uprising, Christmas came and went with little disturbance. The freedmen, disappointed in their hopes, redoubled efforts to seek their own solutions.

Physical violence was the most inflammatory plantation abuse. Ex-Confederate general Josiah Gorgas saw a white carrying a whip while transporting hands three months after Appomattox. Months later a Mississippi newspaper noted "several plantations where the overseers inflict corporal punishment on the negroes," adding that the freedmen were benefited thereby. Private correspondence suggests these issues persisted. The son of North Carolina politician William A. Graham wrote, "I have some difficulty with the negroes in past ten days. The little ones were pretty impudent and I whipped them. Their Mother had a good deal to say about it & they [misbehaved] again. I whipped them again & the boy we have in the house & old man Dick Jesse ran away." He then recovered the elderly escapee, whipping him just to show who was in charge. Given the habits of the old regime, the presence of Freedmen's Bureau agents provided a bracing corrective. If army policies provided one positive message, it was that the days of the lash were over. Reports of whipping supported by physical evidence often yielded arrests. It happened enough to attract notice, and it infuriated planters when it did.

The role of the military, and the Freedmen's Bureau specifically, was double-edged. The Bureau's leadership emphasized that liberation couldn't mean license. For the time being, the freedmen—and freedwomen too—should work as wage laborers. Backed by the prestige of the Northern triumph, many agents, along with army officers, missionaries, teachers, even investors, saw their role as implanting free-labor ideas on a benighted region. The vehicle was the written contract, with standardized provisions protecting the freedmen's interest, to be individually approved and enforced by the Bureau's agents. The head of the household often signed, which embodied the changes in family structure the Bureau hoped to encourage. Contracts generally provided for perhaps ten dollars a month for prime male laborers, with food, housing, and medical care for laborers and their dependents. Work time lost would be deducted from pay. These provisions, the officers hoped, pointed toward full freedom.

Planters increasingly resented the Freedmen's Bureau, but the agency's goals intersected with planters' priorities. Black Codes forced contracts upon the laborers on pain of arrest, while Bureau policy nudged them more gently in the same direction. For freedpeople the prospect was still gang labor and tight supervision by overseers and drivers; in practice not all that much would change save the promise of pay and the absence of the whip. But that absence proved crucial: people would not work like slaves without physical compulsion. Planters universally complained that freedpeople left work whenever short-term opportunities appeared. Hands reportedly neglected maintenance that didn't directly contribute to their crop share, whatever the contract provisions said. Women came and went when they chose, doing just enough to collect their food allotment, and it was difficult to punish them without antagonizing prime male laborers. The employers could deduct from salary at year's end, but too free use of this device made it difficult to hire workers. Bureau agents exhorted the hands to greater exertion, but neither they nor the ex-masters could accomplish much without coercion.

Wretched crops ensued in 1865. Planters widely complained that they had lost money, among them thousands of Northern veterans who invested in Southern plantations. Most white observers blamed the freedpeople's work habits, though the postwar disorder had much to do with it. One result was that the freedpeople seldom made much beyond food and housing for their year's labor. The inexperienced freedmen, who reportedly didn't fully grasp how fractions and collective shares worked, were taken advantage of by hard-pressed planters. The freedmen's portion tended to be laughably low, an eighth or a tenth of the crop, and the hands often found themselves in debt for deducted time. Those working for cash did better, on paper, but laborers had trouble getting paid. Complaints of fraud are rampant in the Freedmen's Bureau correspondence. The hands were bitterly disappointed, which exacerbated their widespread reluctance to sign new contracts and also fed the rumors of confiscation at Christmas.

Things worked out similarly in 1866, save that the freedmen became less tractable. In Greenville, South Carolina, John De Forrest was "called upon to arrange a hundred or two of disputes" that year. The Bureau agent doubted that many were being defrauded, but the freedpeople certainly thought so. De

Forest described a frustrating morning spent with a couple going over their employer's accounts; the books looked right, but they could not be persuaded that their year's labor came to nothing. After another wretched crop, freedpeople looked for some alternative. They tried to rent land independently, but white community pressure and the Black Codes discouraged the practice. Numbers migrated to the cities, but this could hardly absorb the whole rural population.

By early 1867 planters approached bankruptcy. Land prices sunk to as little as a fifth of their prewar value. Many spoke of abandoning production entirely, and wages declined dramatically. For the freedpeople, the mood was even bleaker. A Mississippi planter wrote, "The poor creatures are much disappointed and I think dissatisfied with the result." At this fateful moment national political developments intersected with the agrarian deadlock. In March 1867 Congress decreed black suffrage. There would be a sequence of voter registrations and elections to create new state constitutions. For most states this meant three election campaigns in a bit over a year. The region would be a stew of agitation through the next presidential election. Before Military Reconstruction there had been some organizational efforts among freedpeople, especially in the cities. Now enfranchisement would transform the rural South.

The vehicle of mass politicization would be the Union or Loyal League, a wartime patriotic organization. Congressional Republicans, fearing the influence of the ex-masters, thought this existing group would make an effective teaching medium. The Union League was an oath-bound club, a Republican analogue of the fraternal Masons. Initiates swore to vote for loyal men, and much of the meeting time was occupied with explanations of Reconstruction and the mechanics of casting ballots. Bureau agents and other Northerners, Unconditional Unionists, and some African Americans scattered through the countryside, swearing in members and setting up councils. The appeal was exemplified by a model dialogue between a white Republican and a freedman, reportedly written by the black politician and minister Henry M. Turner. The implication was that outsiders would provide political instruction, and the text was commonly read aloud. The white adviser explained that Lincoln had been a Republican, that his party had enacted voting rights, and that Andrew Johnson was the enemy. One repeated emphasis is on the threat of reenslavement, that freedmen should "shun the Democratic party as they would the overseer's lash and the auction block." After hearing this litany, the fictional freedman sagely responded: "You have clearly shown me my duty and I shall impart the information to my people."

Southern Democrats, and generations of historians after them, viewed Union League rhetoric as demonstrating the gullibility of the freedpeople. Democrats spent significant time denying reenslavement charges. Some ex-Confederates argued that they themselves had been the real liberators, since they forced emancipation upon the reluctant Lincoln. This extravagant bid for gratitude notwithstanding, the effectiveness of the charge likely illustrated the freedmen's acuity rather than ignorance. Reenslavement talk served as an effective metaphor for life under the Black Codes. What else could slavery have meant but gang labor, overseers, and women and children in the workforce? Freedmen applied the Republican rhetoric of equality to their concrete situation and found their circumstances intolerable. As one unreflective Democrat complained, the freedmen wouldn't even listen to him: "prejudice and hate seem to have taken possession of their minds, and excluded the friendly feelings to which a state of slavery gave rise. . . ."

Rural agitation exploded. Scores or even hundreds turned out for the evening Union League gatherings, which were generally held weekly in secluded locations. Whites could seldom locate them, and the format encouraged freedmen to speak their minds. Secret meetings were safer than public rallies, which were frequently broken up by hecklers or gunfire. The League simultaneously became the perfect medium for politics and agrarian agitation, concerns that were not that distinct for freedmen anyway. Radical rhetoric reached people precisely because they were so frustrated as laborers, and the resulting mobilization transformed the countryside. Shadowy reports proliferated of black militias drilling under arms, transforming the balance of fear. Jittery whites misread the freedpeople's intentions as insurrectionary, for their actual conduct was relatively restrained. Radical speeches abounded, and sometimes threats of retaliation, but the whole point of the League was to keep hostile whites away.

Chaotic circumstances disrupted plantation production. At Greensboro, Alabama, a black activist was murdered by a white storeowner who then escaped. Leaguers marched in from the countryside, thousands strong, with some participants threatening to burn the town. Faced with the armed throng, the sheriff essentially *deputized* the crowd. Bands of freedmen searched the countryside, eventually dragging one suspicious fellow to town for punishment. As this went on, whites threatened battle, despite the area's three-to-one black majority. The impact of this incident on the spring crop can be imagined. One overseer complained that his hands "were so much excited they have done but little work" for a week. In September he observed that he still could get little done because of so much politics. Another overseer observed that his hands wouldn't work well, and some told him they were to "have the land and the growing crop upon it . . . they all belong to the u[n]ion league."

Similar episodes proliferated. Renewed talk of "forty acres and a mule" circulated in League meetings, expressing anticipation of drastic change. Political activities disrupted work, and still more did the threat of physical confrontations. Another wretched crop year followed in 1867, with widespread privation. One Mississippian wrote that the blacks were worse off than in the preceding dreadful year. The anxious Yankee general E. O. C. Ord warned of a full-scale insurrection in Mississippi. A woman feared there would be "serious trouble with the Negroes in the country, many of whom are roaming around like Indians." She urged her widowed mother to leave the Georgia countryside for safer quarters.

Many landowners refused to contract for another season, but an increase in the price of cotton early in 1868 broke the stalemate. Planters began renting farms, either to squads of freedpeople, or, increasingly, to individual families laboring under their own direction. One North Carolina plantation manager noted a preference for separate farms, but failing that, freedmen were "anxious to work in different companies." Decentralized tenant farming spread rapidly across most of the cotton South. There were various forms of tenancy, but family-based "sharecropping" became the norm—with the planter providing everything but the labor and taking half the crop as his share. Under these new arrangements, the freedmen went to work and raised better crops. Relieved landowners finally put the postwar specter of ruin behind them.

By the early 1870s the transition to family-based tenant farming was well under way in cotton. Sharecropping might have emerged anyway, but the politicization of the freedpeople sped the process. Now black men and women would no longer work under direct supervision, which minimized the possibility of whipping; family members would determine who would work and how much. The residual practices of slavery changed, for good or ill; tenants were responsible for feeding themselves, or, in practice, borrowing the money to do so. Even the physical geography of the plantations changed. The freedpeople dismantled the old slave quarters and built dispersed cabins alongside their own crops. This made it easier for them to own pigs and chickens, and it gave families privacy too. Freedpeople continued to work on white people's land; in 1870 black rural families outnumbered landowners twenty to one in South Carolina, fifty to one in Alabama. Still, the changes seemed like an improvement, concessions in the direction of black autonomy. This stabilized the plantation system, and in the ensuing years strikes and labor unrest became far less common.

Outside the cotton region, similar forces were at work. In the Upper South tobacco similarly evolved toward sharecropping, though the process took longer. In sugar, with its highly centralized production regime, planters persisted with gang labor. They did so by paying laborers more than they could make elsewhere. But if the south Louisiana planters maintained traditional methods, they also faced continuing work stoppages and bloody confrontations continuing well after Reconstruction. In coastal South Carolina and Georgia, plantation production declined, with the freedpeople of the sea islands eventually gaining significant amounts of deteriorating land. On the nearby mainland, rice planters who persisted in large-scale production faced continuing labor turmoil. Politically tinged wage disputes continued in low-country South Carolina throughout Reconstruction.

There was one crucial drawback to the breakup of the old plantation system: it antagonized white neighbors while rendering the tenants physically less secure. The spatial geography of the plantations changed, for sharecroppers' cabins were increasingly scattered throughout the landscape. When concentrated in the old slave quarters, sheer numbers provided some protection from violence. Tenants were now more vulnerable, at least in areas where African Americans did not vastly predominate. This contributed to the worst terrorist episode in American history, the emergence of the Ku Klux Klan and a host of similar groups.

Numerous precedents existed, for slavery encouraged vigilantism. Recent scholars have found that slaves received a degree of due process in antebellum courts, but in urgent circumstances whites lynched or tortured suspects without obstruction. The antebellum patrol system was another antecedent, for white men were periodically expected to ride the roads at night and whip slaves without passes. These hated "patterollers" had an unsavory association with lawless poor whites. Harriet Jacobs, for example, recalled uncouth patrollers bursting into her grandmother's home after the Nat Turner insurrection. If whites were vigilant before the war, the level of alarm only increased afterward. Union authorities forbade formal militias, but many whites perceived some such system as a necessity. Extralegal patrols, occasionally in disguise, were riding in some areas even before Military Reconstruction. And emancipation weakened the financial incentive for elite whites to protect blacks from random violence.

The Civil War itself encouraged violence. Vast numbers served in the Confederate army. The war transformed a whole generation into proficient killers, skilled with firearms and used to following orders, many specifically trained as cavalry. Bands of Confederate partisans or "bushwhackers" operated behind the federal lines, employing many of the skills Klansmen would use. After the war, partisan units were sometimes reconstituted under the same leadership. A spontaneous wealth of Confederate military experience was available, a familiarity freedpeople generally did not have. Whites also generally had horses and better weapons. As the Democratic journalist Edward Pollard explained on the eve of the Klan explosion, "The population of the South is peculiar. . . . They are a ready-made army."

Then there was the experience of racial mastery, the confidence born of ordering people around. White Southerners often invoked such psychological explanations. Eliza Frances Andrews of Georgia might logically have been fearful after the

Klan shot up a Republican rally, but she crudely dismissed the notion of resistance. "The negroes are very much exasperated," she observed, "but the poor creatures are too stupid and defenseless to do any harm: they do not know how to organize for their own defense." More than a decade after emancipation, one South Carolinian observed, "The negroes yet retain their inbred dread of their old masters, and their old inbred dread of *striking whites*," while the whites retained "their native contempt . . . and readiness to dash on the blacks." Throughout Reconstruction, Southern whites normally prevailed in armed showdowns if the numbers were anywhere near even—with casualty counts running five and ten to one. It would be difficult to find people better equipped to undertake repression.

Historians have argued over the extent that terror was focused on partisan goals or on wider social and economic objectives. This makes sense in analyzing a decentralized popular movement. The consensus is that it was political in the broad sense, counteracting all the changes brought by emancipation and Military Reconstruction. Most Southern whites honestly believed black suffrage outrageous. One North Carolinian pondered emigration because "any place is to be preferred to one which exposes us to the equality and savage rule of the colored race." Ex-Governor James Orr of South Carolina, himself somehow an eventual Republican, called it "the most solemn farce that has been enacted in all history." Talk of race war became pervasive. Later Klan apologists blamed taxation or corruption for provoking the movement. But the timing is wrong to explain the expansion of the Klan across the South in early 1868; the installation of Reconstruction civil governments was still months away. The unfolding of Military Reconstruction itself, combined with the changes in agricultural organization, provided the impetus.

Counteracting black enfranchisement was the concrete objective, the most politically focused goal. But whites perceived emancipation in general as the problem—the loss of control. The devolution of the centralized plantation was one piece of the process, despite the odd circumstance that the Klan spread just as cotton prices rose and production improved. The Klan's motivations were as broad as the global social challenge that Southern whites perceived. A published Klan ritual queried prospective members if they favored a white man's government. It asked, "Are you opposed to negro equality, both social and political?" Similarly, the Knights of the White Camelia, a terrorist group centered in Louisiana, emphasized only two phrases in its long initiation: "MAINTENANCE OF THE SUPREMACY OF THE WHITE RACE" and observing "A MARKED DISTINCTION BETWEEN THE TWO RACES." Thus terrorists shot and intimidated political leaders and voters, but they also disarmed freedmen by the hundred, punished accused thieves and criminals, burned schools and churches. They acted on innumerable private grudges too. Terrorists sought to restore racial subordination in all the ways that status had been challenged.

The Klan's organizational history is murky. In Pulaski, Tennessee, in 1866, a group of Confederate veterans formed a social club, something along the lines of a fraternity with pseudo-Greek rigmarole. It apparently had no political overtones—though that point is disputed—but as Brownlow's government enacted black suffrage in 1867, the passwords and outfits were pressed into political service in Tennessee, spreading across the region the following year. The order's array of Dragons, Genii, and Hydras had attractive features, for Klan activities could be excused as hijinks or practical jokes. As Albion Tourgée bitterly recalled, "The nation held its sides with laughter, and the Ku-Klux took heart from these cheerful echoes. . . ." Another Republican recalled humorous Klan-themed floats in Northern parades. Apologists claimed the disguises played on the freedmen's fear of ghosts, enabling intimidation without unseemly violence. Whatever the likelihood of this, the plausibility furnished political cover.

Ex-Confederate general Nathan Bedford Forrest was the widely reported leader of the Klan. He received "fifty to one hundred letters a day and had a private secretary writing all the time," and his travels as an insurance executive furthered the organization's spread. In March and April 1868, during the impeachment trial of Andrew Johnson, flamboyant Klan threats sprouted in the region's Democratic newspapers. Ryland Randolph, editor of the *Tuscaloosa Monitor*, later stated that he wrote the Klan notices in his paper, which would make sense given his admitted leadership of the county Klan. In the Southern Democratic press, in the heat of the presidential campaign, the Klan could do no wrong. Few expressed misgivings in public, and they were uncommon even in private.

As a region-wide formal entity, the Klan had only a brief life, about a year. One might conceptualize the Klan as a terrorist technique rather than an actual organization. A dozen or more horsemen, with themselves and mounts disguised, would ride to individual cabins in the dead of night, disarming, whipping, or killing as circumstances dictated. Klansmen were available to alibi one another, and raiders were often called in from a distance to frustrate identification. With the army force available, it was difficult to counteract this scheme or identify perpetrators after the fact. If victims ambushed Klansmen, as sometimes happened, the heroic would confront hundreds of night riders on successive evenings. And even if Klansmen were apprehended, they would be tried in local courts where a single sympathizer could prevent conviction. Almost no one of the Klan was ever punished by Southern courts, even under Republican state governments. The main individual recourse for the freedpeople was to sleep out in the woods, or to abandon the crop and flee, unsatisfactory responses that vast numbers employed.

But who were the terrorists? This issue is closely tied to the issue of motivation, and it is complicated by the evolving composition of the movement. Forms of involvement varied, from passive enablers to violent perpetrators. Night-riding participants were younger men, many teenaged, and primarily Confederate veterans. In terms of social composition, the terrorist movement seems broadly based among rural native whites, both in numbers and class background. Forrest reportedly claimed he could turn out forty thousand armed members in Tennessee, and North Carolina Democrats seeking amnesty later claimed similar numbers. Of course one cannot readily distinguish between formal Klan members and the multitudes of kindred groups or clusters of individuals. Overall the terrorist participants must have numbered in the tens of thousands, probably more. It was so pervasive because members believed it morally justified. As the Republican Albion Tourgée later conceded, thousands cooperated in the belief they were "acting in self-defense in so doing, and especially that they were securing the safety of their wives and children thereby." A federal prosecution official in South Carolina came to the same conclusion. Beyond this, partisan motives were most evident early on: the movement was promoted by Democratic politicians, lawyers, and editors, smarting under disfranchisement. Klan apologists stressed upper-class support, which at first looks true, especially where raids dovetailed into guerrilla conflict with highland Unionists.

The initial results looked favorable for Reconstruction's opponents. The Klan's timing was propitious, just as military oversight gave way to civilian rule. "Anarchy is surely impending," one Union officer foretold. In plantation areas the Klan returned the balance of fear to whites' favor, at least where blacks did not vastly predominate. Terrorists demolished the Union League, repressing the agrarian mobilization behind it. Republican leaders often disbanded the organization themselves. The Klan thus held promise as an instrument of vote suppression. The success suggested that Congressional Reconstruction could be reversed if the Democrats carried the next national election.

In 1868 the unabashed neo-Confederate viewpoint associated with terrorism posed a problem for national Democrats. Popular enthusiasm encouraged incautious behavior. The mobilization might help locally, but it was bad public relations in a presidential election year. "Waving the bloody shirt"—literally of Klan victims—brought the whole rebellion back, making Northerners' own racial attitudes beside the point. After U. S. Grant's election gave the entire federal government to the Republicans, dispirited Southern whites took stock, especially former conservatives who perceived that Democratic zealots had done them in yet again. A chastened General Forrest issued repeated public orders disbanding the Klan. This may have been a subterfuge, but many of the political leaders and planters dropped out. Organized terror remained evident in some state elections, but more moderate conservatives increasingly sought deniability. As the partisan rationale unraveled, the Klan ceased to exist as a region-wide political movement, but the terror only escalated in ferocity. It became simple racial mayhem, with a more tenuous connection to electoral considerations.

Emancipation had raised a host of grievances, and the Klan technique responded to all of them. The political motive predominated, but in social terms the changes in the plantation system were crucial. As tenant farming spread, whites perceived a loss of racial control. Less prosperous white landowners and tenants experienced all of the resulting inconveniences with few of the compensations. Traditionally, farmers allowed their livestock, especially hogs, to rove freely through the unfenced woodland. Theft was endemic to plantation life, but since slaves were under close control, access remained limited. Now the freedpeople had guns and dogs, and as tenants they were left to provision themselves. Complaints of property theft proliferated. Planters obsessed about the problem, but they had increasing crop production to console them. For neighboring farmers, losses were hard to bear.

Octavia Otey, a widow living near Huntsville, Alabama, offers one of the few diary accounts of Klan operations. After she reluctantly rented land to the freedpeople in 1868, she reported increasing theft, and her neighbors began inquiring about vanishing livestock. She soon heard of Klansmen conducting a crossroads trial of accused thieves, whipping one brutally. Disguised horsemen appeared at her place, asking if the freedpeople were "humble and respectful" to her, and promising protection. They demanded one hand by name, a request she evaded, and the man escaped. Otey thought she knew the night riders and perceived their intrusion as well intentioned. Horsemen returned several times during the subsequent winter, and by then the elections were long over. The evident motive was to bolster the widow lady and thus counteract a neighborhood problem.

As the terrorist movement decentralized, it became more identified with the concerns of white small farmers and tenants. No mechanism existed to control the violence; any white could assail blacks with near impunity, confident that community sentiment would protect him. Calculations of electoral expediency became less evident. To take one example, nearly four hundred accused terrorists were identified in Alabama, mostly charged by the federal government in the early 1870s. It was possible to locate some ninety in the census, and of them only two had more than five thousand dollars in real property. Well over a third reported no property at all. Many were young men in their late teens and early twenties, with the majority owning no land. What the terrorists did possess was mostly held in pigs and cattle, the very property most susceptible to the plantation changes. In addition, white tenants sometimes expelled rivals for access to land.

As time went on, elites became more wary of unrestrained terror, even in places where the political motivation was long evident. Late in 1870, Eliza Frances Andrews of Georgia was critical of Klansmen for shooting up a Republican rally. Although the leaders were in her social circle, her diary observed: "They ought to be ashamed of themselves—at least Charley ought, but I don't believe Dudley DuBose has sense enough to know there is anything disgraceful in heading a gang of rowdies and assassins." In western North Carolina, Klan leader Randolph Shotwell recalled being told by the Democratic leadership to rein in the violence, just after federal anti-terrorist legislation in early 1871. He hoped to exercise restraint, because the farmers "knew me to be of a different class than themselves," and his intention was to put the choice of targets under outside direction. But he found himself unable to control the "headstrong, unmanageable scamps—who committed all the deeds of which the Order should really be ashamed." His failure would secure him a stay in federal prison.

The terrorist campaign could not reverse the changes in agricultural practices that were already under way, but they did still the wave of agrarian unrest. Emancipation had engendered social conflict over gang labor and similar holdovers of slavery, and, briefly, black politicization had altered the social balance. Had the situation persisted, further changes in agriculture might have occurred, or at least the laborers' bargaining position would have been better. The terror campaign forestalled that possibility, restoring the balance of intimidation in whites' favor. By the 1870s many planters concluded that renting out land wasn't so bad, especially since they kept the books. They mourned the loss of authority, but money talked. The freedpeople lost their illusions but had few alternatives, and at least their day-to-day reality had changed in gratifying ways. Labor conflict lessened, and the plantation system resolidified for decades. The stabilization of plantation agriculture, with a balkanized workforce, shifted struggle to the political sphere.

As a political phenomenon, the Klan and kindred organizations met with mixed success. They wrought havoc locally, but they also handed the federal government over to the Republicans. This meant that the newly established Reconstruction governments became operational, under new constitutions, with the legal authority to tax and enact legislation. This failure left formal power in the hands of the desperate victims of terrorist violence. Because the Klan had been effective in stopping rural change, it was in the formal political process that remaining hopes for change would unfold.

4

Establishing the Reconstruction Governments

AS THE POSTWAR plantation struggles played out, and before the Klan movement hit stride, a drastic governmental transformation was under way. In March 1867 Congress took control of Reconstruction, incorporating African Americans as voters and disfranchising thousands of former officeholders. Congressional or "Radical" Reconstruction temporarily removed the old ruling class from power, allowing the most disaffected elements in Southern society to come to the fore. Republican leaders in the South could now try to institutionalize democratic change and safeguard core interests of civil rights and loyal rule. Along with enacting new constitutions, they also sought a competitive Republican party, strong enough to defend the interests of its constituents.

The congressional architects of Reconstruction saw grounds for optimism. No one imagined the terrorist resistance to come, and black suffrage won support precisely because it seemed so simple. As James Garfield recalled, Congress rejected "constant interference with the local laws of the States" in favor of giving freedmen political means of self-defense. Frederick Douglass and other abolitionists made similar arguments of convenience, and for better or worse these prevailed. In the ex-Confederate states, freedpeople represented about 40 percent of the population. Manhood suffrage alone might bring Republicans close to winning fair elections under federal protection. Congressional leaders assumed that African Americans were naturally Republican, and they were right, though the pattern proved more complex than anticipated. Internal fissures became important within factional politics, but they only occasionally interfered with near-unanimous Republican ballots.

Securing the freedmen's vote solved only part of the problem. In just two states did blacks represent a clear majority of the population, South Carolina (59 percent) and Mississippi (55 percent), though they had about even numbers in Louisiana (50 percent-plus) and Florida (49 percent). In most of the ten Reconstructed states, a substantial white vote was necessary for the success of the Republican program. The theoretical possibility of an African-American majority is misleading anyway, because Northerners were unenthusiastic about voting by propertyless and illiterate freedmen. As one congressman observed, "Where it is all black on one side and white on the other, I see no safety." *The Nation*, while backing Reconstruction, nonetheless observed that "the complete supremacy of the negro in some of the Southern States is extremely repulsive to many Republicans, and it is deprecated by many more." The journal observed that Southern whites ought to be welcomed to the party and given influence in proportion to their numbers in the population. Equal suffrage so depended on federal protection that these preferences could not be ignored.

But where were white votes to come from, given that the Republicans were the regional anathema? After all, Republican victory in 1860 had prompted secession. The party remained identified with the Yankee cause and protection of the former slaves, and for these substantial reasons it was reviled. Only those alienated from the regional consensus could find such an alliance acceptable. The one substantial white constituency for Reconstruction was among the Unconditional Unionists, concentrated in the region's mountains and hills. An estimated hundred thousand whites had joined the Union army, and draft resisters had dominated many up-country locales. But the return of Confederate veterans often transformed loyalists into a beleaguered minority. People on both sides had violent scores to settle. Control of local government and juries became crucial matters as people indicted one another for wartime deeds; in some places partisans used the courts to drive out unwelcome neighbors. In Unionist-dominated east Tennessee, for example, Governor Brownlow essentially told ex-Confederates to stay away because he would not protect them. Even food relief became politicized because distribution occurred through local officials or Bureau agents. Unionist dissidents felt betrayed by their former hero, Andrew Johnson, whose policies restored ex-Confederates to local power.

W. E. B. Du Bois once characterized Reconstruction as an experiment in biracial popular democracy. Most white voters supporting Reconstruction indeed came from the up-country, in the nonplantation areas. They were not necessarily poorer than their neighbors, but they were concentrated in the less prosperous reaches of the South. Unionists often signed documents with an illiterate cross, a class marker which suggests intellectual isolation. Native white Republican voters—scoundrelly "scalawags" as the slur went—defined themselves against the slaveholding secessionists. At the constitutional conventions, poorer delegates would be conspicuous as white "Radicals." Their class animus was reflected in Reconstruction politics, especially on debt relief issues, because so many up-country people were in dire need.

One can conceptualize Reconstruction as a lower-class interracial alliance, but economic equality issues per se never gained much traction with the wider public. The needs of white farmers potentially conflicted with those of the plantation gentry, as the later agrarian revolt against Democratic rule demonstrated. Some scholars have argued that a reform politics anticipating the Populists might have succeeded, but it is difficult to imagine how, given the national configuration. Republicans were wholly identified with activist government, and Jacksonian hostility to such policies traditionally influenced up-country politics, especially among poorer farmers. It took decades for accumulated grievances to reorient agrarians' thinking toward the state. Courting small farmers would have been difficult anyway, given Southern Republicans' dependence on the business-minded national party, and more fundamentally the passions of the war interfered. The Confederate army was mostly composed of nonslaveholders, and wartime loyalties cut a jagged gash across class-based politics.

Unconditional Unionists were a crucial constituency, in several states enough to combine with blacks and comprise an electoral majority. They became the numerical backbone of white Republican support. But they came with liabilities, because they were perhaps more urgently resented than the freedpeople themselves. The Unionist government in Tennessee, which disfranchised most ex-Confederate voters, emphasized the depth of their alienation. Governor Brownlow proclaimed that Rebels had "forfeited all rights to citizenship, and to life itself." In Northern eyes, the Unconditional Unionist leaders presented an uncomfortably narrow and intransigent image. One sympathetic newspaper warned Brownlow upon inauguration that he had to tone down his rhetoric. The *New York Times* characterized his followers as "ruffians and cutthroats." In the spring of 1867 some Unconditional Unionists endorsed Thaddeus Stevens's proposal to confiscate Rebel lands, or they sounded socially radical in other ways. Beyond this, the issue of wartime loyalty would inevitably recede over time, both with the Northern public and within the South itself.

National Republican leaders sought a broader cross section
of white support. The congressional architects of Reconstruction
were not generally Radicals like Stevens or Sumner, men who
envisioned a social transformation of the South—that is, beyond
equality and loyal rule. Congressional leaders instead felt they
had to have acquiescence from some former Confederates. Reconstruction legislation was premised on substantial white participation in creating new constitutions, for fear the new regimes
might be extravagantly radical. In particular the business-
minded Republicans who would promote Grant for president
sought ballast. The accessions most desired were perhaps
"Union" men, but not like Brownlow or Holden. They tended to
be prewar conservatives, as the contemporary terminology went,
who had reluctantly acquiesced to the Confederacy. When postwar Southern-rights Democrats reasserted themselves, these
men were alienated anew, especially those with political ambi-
tions. A recent study of eight hundred prominent scalawags reveals that while many were prosperous men who had backed the
Confederacy, they had opposed immediate secession overwhelmingly.

The former Whigs especially had points of logical congru-
ence with the national Republicans. The Whigs were strongest
among prosperous urbanites and the established slaveholders of
the plantation belt. These men often perceived secession in elitist
terms, as Democratic extremists whipping up popular sentiment.
The antebellum Whigs favored activist government to foster
commerce through internal improvements, public education,
and subsidies for business enterprise. Whigs also favored a pro-
tective tariff, a matter of urgency for south Louisiana's once-rich
sugar planters, as was levee rebuilding. With the region in ruins,
infrastructure spending seemed all the more pressing. National
Republicans favored economic development programs, especially for railroads, and they were in a position to implement

their policies. For ex-Whigs, the possibility of using Reconstruction to reanimate stalled initiatives beckoned.

Given the pariah status of the Republicans, few former Whigs rushed to affiliate openly. There were, however, degrees of complicity in the Congressional Reconstruction process, or at least degrees of opposition. Some would convert quietly once the Reconstruction governments were installed and President Grant's election suggested permanence. For individuals with political aspirations, especially those in financial difficulties, participation in Reconstruction offered a personal way out. Most Southern Republicans were so poor that a man with upper-class attributes could rise quickly. James Lusk Alcorn called himself perhaps the largest planter in Mississippi. Alcorn would be elected as the state's first Republican governor, profiled in *Harper's Weekly*. Such an elite pedigree made one stand out in Republican politics. One South Carolina newcomer, Louis Post, remembered his "boyish thrill" at meeting ex-governor James Orr, an old regime figure turned Republican judge. He similarly recalled future governor Franklin Moses as "an old-time Jewish aristocrat."

Almost all native white Republicans saw themselves as Union men by some definition, out of sympathy with regional trends. One group of whites, however, were literally outsiders. Prewar arrivals from the North or overseas, many of them merchants or tradesmen in the region's cities, had often opposed secession. They functioned as a surprisingly open dissident subculture, shielded by business connections. Another contingent literally came southward in the wake of the Union army, often federal soldiers with relevant professional experience. Officers and chaplains in the United States Colored Infantry were well placed to enter politics. Many Northerners came as missionaries, teachers, or Freedmen's Bureau agents. Other newcomers had a different profile, investing in plantations. Land was cheap by antebellum standards, so veterans often committed their wartime savings.

One *New York Tribune* reporter hailed the influx to the South, predicting that "wealth will be poured into the lap of the newcomers." An estimated twenty to fifty thousand Northerners relocated after the war. Once in the South, though, they shared in the general plantation disaster. Most returned home, but Congressional Reconstruction opened timely career opportunities for those willing to brave white disfavor. As Henry Clay Warmoth observed of "hundreds, if not thousands" of his fellow veterans in Louisiana, "All of us were soon up to our eyes in politics, made so by conditions which none of us could control."

Newcomers were not numerous among the electorate, but they were prominent in the Republican leadership. Of the delegates to the constitutional conventions, some 17 percent were recent arrivals, a vast overrepresentation of their numbers, and they preponderantly represented black constituencies. The widespread stereotype of such men as "carpetbaggers" (named for a form of luggage, with the implication they were transient freebooters) misleads in several respects. Almost all arrived before black suffrage seemed likely. Many were former officers, with the class and educational status that implies, but they were young men in a hurry, their careers having been sidetracked by the war. Future U.S. senator George Spencer headed south because he thought "the chances of making a fortune there the best," but he interrupted his Alabama career for several months to pursue opportunities in California. Northern connections helped such men rise into leadership ranks, but their appeal to the freedpeople was crucial. While they had the full range of Northern racial prejudice, they also saw themselves as the downtrodden blacks' defenders. As one Republican editor privately observed, many of the newcomers in Tennessee were strongly anti-slavery in sentiment. They were "more ready to sustain new rights or claim new privileges for the blacks" and thus gained their confidence. Conversely, prewar Southern politicians necessarily made pro-slavery declarations, and their very former prominence tainted them before the new electorate.

These diverse constituencies came together at state Republican gatherings before the constitutional conventions met. All supported loyal rule and civil rights in broad terms and called for an expansion of public education. Humanitarian reforms were endorsed, like abolishing corporal punishment and imprisonment for debt. On economic matters, Republicans called vaguely for taxation policies to democratize the land structure and expanded homestead debt exemptions. Several party statements also promised to promote corporate enterprise. Virginia's Republicans promised to weaken usury laws to encourage outside investment. South Carolina would promote "a liberal system of public improvements, such as railroads, canal and other works," and other Republican meetings made similar pledges.

Beyond the Republican ranks there was also pragmatic white support for participation in the Reconstruction process, as a final settlement that Congress would accept. Some whites perceived that refraining was dangerous. Robert E. Lee himself suggested that whites ought to register and vote for good men if they could. The existence of "Reconstructionist" conservatives muddied the political lines and thus furthered the initial steps in the process. In Georgia one-third of the registered whites voted to reconstruct on Congress's terms. In Alabama and North Carolina it was around 30 percent. In all ten states the electorate authorized new constitutions, aided by disproportionate initial black registration. Republicans dominated all these gatherings save perhaps Georgia, so they were in a position to implement their priorities. From late 1867 through the early months of 1868, the constitutional conventions became the most important political arena.

Of the more than 1,000 delegates elected, native Southern whites were the most numerous bloc, numbering nearly 600, split evenly between unconditional Unionists and those of more conservative inclination. Recent migrants from the North were also conspicuous. African Americans numbered about 268, less than their portion of the population and vastly below their share of the Republican electorate. Only in one state, South Carolina, did blacks hold a substantial majority, around 76 of 124 delegates, though in Louisiana they held a slight majority under a party policy that they be allocated half the nominations. These two states with major urban centers also had the largest number of educated African Americans. South Carolina, for example, drew a number from the North, some with missionary society or abolitionist backgrounds. Similarly in Louisiana, one study found that a striking 85 percent with known origins were former free people of color, many of them from the privileged Afro-Creole caste. These attributes influenced constitutional developments in these two states, but everywhere else African Americans were a decided minority, and former slaves were more numerous among the delegates. Under these more typical circumstances, activists deferred readily to their white allies.

Democrats nationwide heaped racist scorn on these conventions. By contrast, most modern scholars, and even some of the turn-of-the-century Dunning school, conclude that these constitutions were competently written. For example, ex-governor Daniel Chamberlain disavowed Reconstruction many decades later, but even he recalled that South Carolina drafted "a fairly good constitution." The document remained in effect until 1895, and Virginia's constitution lasted until 1902, suggesting that even those who overthrew Reconstruction saw few urgent defects. *Harper's Weekly* noted that the new documents "resemble in general form and phraseology the Constitutions of all the other States, and in some respects are superior to those now in force elsewhere."

The most contentious debates arose over disfranchising former Rebels and proscribing the old ruling class from office. This

was the defining "Radical" demand, generating far more national discussion than civil rights provisions. With the proposed
Fourteenth Amendment, Congress proscribed former officials
who had backed the Confederacy, and the Reconstruction acts
temporarily disfranchised them, so many Southern Republicans
saw a mandate. Also, they had the example of the Brownlow
government in Tennessee, which swept the polls by a wide margin in August 1867. Wartime Unionists everywhere opposed ex-
Confederate political participation, at least for the time being;
they wanted offices immediately vacated and filled with loyal appointees. Black suffrage didn't change the electorate much outside the plantation regions, and if up-country loyalists wanted
control locally, they had to purge the existing electorate. Strong
Unionists also sought symbolic vindication, a public stigma for
ex-secessionist leaders. In Texas many Unionists wanted the acts
under the Confederate regime declared void *ab initio*—from the
beginning. This would have thrown out all judicial decisions and
voided existing railroad land grants. These policies would have
spread legal confusion but also improved the state's finances, salvaged the school fund, and made land available for settlers. This
issue, along with a Radical proposal to divide Texas to create a
solidly Union mini-state, stalled the constitutional process for
years.

Others thought too much disfranchisement of ex-Confederate
voters was counterproductive. It stigmatized mild conservatives
who had not gone into open rebellion against the Confederacy,
which was indeed the inclination for those boasting more pronounced loyalty—resistance in arms against Confederate authority. Class tensions were evident, because draft resisters were
mostly poorer men whereas many of those with more conservative politics were of prosperous background, part of the old ruling
elite. At the conventions, conservatives were far more prosperous
than native white Radicals. Proscription of ex-Confederates posed

a serious inconvenience for less heroic planter dissidents because
many had escaped military service by seeking local office. These
compromised conservatives now found themselves targeted by the
energized Unconditional Unionists, who thought their moment
had come.

Unconditional Unionist insistence drove the disfranchisement proposals, but the African-American delegates were conflicted. Wartime loyalty was not the freedpeoples' most pressing
concern, but many black delegates trusted the Radical scalawags
and the newcomers who often agreed with them. Emphatic
Unionists called themselves Republican willingly, denounced
slaveholders with vigor, and accepted black suffrage as something other than an unpleasant means to placate Congress. Also,
African Americans could see practical advantages to barring the
plantation elite: it would maximize their electoral influence and
bolster Republican majorities. This was the prevailing sentiment,
though there was ambivalence. Freedmen so predominated in
many plantation areas that a few disfranchised whites wouldn't
matter locally. The black-dominated South Carolina convention,
for example, never pursued such measures. Furthermore the appeal of universal suffrage was impaired if numbers of whites
didn't vote—the symbolic point was for everyone to vote together. One Alabama delegate observed, "I have no desire to take
away any rights of the white man; all I want is equal rights in the
court-house and equal rights when I go to vote."

Resolution came from the congressional leadership. Just as
the Southern constitutional conventions were preparing to meet,
Northern states had off-year elections in the fall of 1867. Republicans lost ground, and equal-suffrage amendments went down
in several states. With President Johnson mostly lying low, the
Northern public demonstrated a lack of enthusiasm for Congressional Reconstruction, or at least a desire to move on to new issues. Radicals like Stevens got the blame, and the electorate

probably found the prospect of governments dominated by his Southern allies unsettling. The editor Horace Greeley, considered a Radical leader, urged Republicans to rein in the Southern conventions. Alabama, the first state to commence the Reconstruction process, received direct pressure. Delegates actually dispatched an emissary to Washington for instructions. Congress would have to readmit the Reconstructed states, so its wishes could not readily be ignored.

This was perhaps a decisive juncture, because Northern sentiment blunted the central initiative of the native Unionist leaders. Whatever the democratic justification for abandoning disfranchisement quickly, it had difficult implications. It sent Democrats back to the polls in the midst of the Klan upsurge, with every prospect of overturning narrow Republican majorities that November. The situation promoted chaos, and a few years more of disfranchisement could hardly have had worse practical consequences. Still, the pragmatists in Congress called the shots. In most Southern states, delegates fell in line, though in Virginia, Arkansas, and Mississippi they disfranchised some ex-Confederates. Northern papers criticized such measures but, as Mississippi's Albert Morgan insisted, "we knew what we were doing." Delegates elsewhere satisfied themselves with indirect means, like several states' requirement that voters swear to recognize civil and political equality. Louisiana discouraged ex-Rebel participation most imaginatively: wartime officeholders, and those who had written treasonable sermons or newspaper articles, were disfranchised—until they filed a recantation of their actions as morally wrong, for publication.

On other issues the delegates found more common ground and better satisfied Northern expectations. Lawmakers repealed the Black Codes, enacting basic civil equality before the law. The presence of so many educated Northerners, especially lawyers, provided experience in constitution-making elsewhere. State bills of rights guaranteed a long list of civil liberties. The new constitutions abolished imprisonment for debt and the whipping post as judicial punishment; they also expanded married women's property rights and, in South Carolina, for the first time provided for divorce procedures. Democratizing reforms were approved in several states: local officials in North Carolina had long been selected by the General Assembly, and lawmakers now made most such positions elective. South Carolina, in particular, had maintained property qualifications for voting and holding office, and the new constitution eliminated those restrictions. In Florida, however, judges were made appointive rather than elective, with the evident intent to insulate these positions from the new electorate, while similar provisions in black-majority South Carolina had precisely the opposite goal.

Florida's constitution declared public schools "the paramount duty of the state," and Republicans everywhere wrote this democratic policy into fundamental law. The war had wrecked existing school systems, and Presidential Reconstruction governments had not provided for educating freedpeople at all. The new constitutions would rectify that, envisioning a permanent increase in state funding. Several constitutions provided that all citizens were entitled to an education up to a certain age. Virginia mandated that every county have schools operational by 1875, and thereafter it was illegal to allow children to grow up in ignorance. In South Carolina several black delegates were educators or missionaries, and some proposed disfranchising illiterates after a lapse of time. Robert Brown Elliott argued for compulsory schooling, hoping to mold white children toward tolerance. The constitution provided for mandatory attendance, eventually, and for six months of classes per year.

Reform aspirations also underlay the most controversial education issue at the South Carolina convention, racial integration. Most black delegates disavowed mandated integration, but a few thought students could learn from one another. More practically, several black delegates wanted the right to attend white schools, to force fair access and funding. "We have not said there shall be no separate schools," the educator Francis L. Cardozo emphasized, but he thought it absurd to bar anyone where few facilities existed. The constitution allowed students to attend whatever public schools or colleges they chose. Louisiana's constitution went beyond this, providing an outright ban on racial exclusion.

One might almost fault the delegates for doing too much for education. Several states authorized poll taxes to support public schools, an ironic provision in view of the subsequent use of the tax. Some scholars also have argued that during Reconstruction, African Americans placed too many of their hopes in public education. Perhaps freedpeople had unrealistic expectations, given their more pressing material needs, and the timing was difficult in view of the region's economic woes. Still, as future governor Adelbert Ames of Mississippi would observe, "Money can never be better expended for education tha[n] at this moment. This generation needs schools as no other generation can." African Americans felt little inclination to wait upon their ex-masters' convenience, and it would be difficult to find a social initiative that enjoyed broader national support. It was redolent of all sorts of Yankee virtues of self-control and temperance, and the public was well aware of the freedpeople's enthusiasm. The press noted reports of freedchildren seeking *summer* schooling, in Louisiana! When property owners bewailed taxes for education, the complaints sounded petty. Horace Greeley was losing enthusiasm for Reconstruction by 1871, but a Southern visit reminded him that the old aristocracy "grudge every penny assessed on them for building school-houses and paying teachers, as though they were to be thrown into the sea." There were other motivations for backing schools, but this priority bid adroitly for Northern sympathy.

Such political circumspection prevailed, even on civil rights. Francis Cardozo cogently observed that "Nearly all the white inhabitants of the State are ready at any moment to deprive us of these rights, and not a loop-hole should be left that would permit them to do it constitutionally." But his colleagues did not pursue this logic, and only in two states did they push civil rights hard. South Carolina's explicit debate of the merits of school integration was one example. In Louisiana's convention, the large contingent of educated freeborn blacks pressed for outright guarantees. The state's constitution provided for nondiscriminatory treatment in transportation, business establishments, and schools. Elsewhere black delegates mostly satisfied themselves with turning back efforts to mandate racial segregation. Doing nothing left the door ajar for future redress.

Thus even on the urgent civil rights issue, African-American leaders deported themselves cautiously. Some carried this policy to surprising lengths. William H. Grey of Arkansas "wanted this a white man's government, and wanted them to do the legislating as they had the intelligence and wealth." Such statements seemed expedient, but it was difficult to know where to draw the line. Georgia's delegates, for example, deliberately avoided an explicit guarantee of the right to hold office. Bishop Henry M. Turner, a future racial militant, endorsed this tactic. When the new legislature met, he and his colleagues, following Congress's lead, voted to admit Democrats apparently barred from office under the Fourteenth Amendment. The Democrats then immediately sought expulsion of black representatives on grounds of racial ineligibility, and aided by a few white Republican renegades, they prevailed. Reconstruction in Georgia dissolved into chaos over this instant betrayal of civil rights.

Delegates commonly deferred to Northern opinion on economic matters. The constitutions reflected solicitude for corporate enterprise, some authorizing state governments to lend credit to railroads. Louisiana's convention debated immediate measures to rebuild the levee system, flooding having ruined many of the state's richest plantations. On the other hand, seldom was the land reform issue even raised. Senator Henry Wilson of Massachusetts warned, "Let confiscation be, as it should be, an unspoken word in your State." Georgia's Aaron Bradley called for such measures, but he was expelled on morals charges. Delegates mostly contented themselves with the hope that homestead legislation and fairer taxation would eventually provide access. In South Carolina, where "forty acres and a mule" had substance, lawmakers did pursue the issue. Aware of the political barriers to direct confiscation, the South Carolina delegates petitioned Congress for a loan of one million dollars to buy land. Republican leaders rebuffed the notion instantly, so the convention authorized a land commission to buy and subdivide plantations. This effort had some success, but it also ran into the sort of corruption that bedeviled even Reconstruction's most positive initiatives.

Economic legislation was crafted primarily for outreach to white voters, especially on the debt issue. Constitutions were drafted after a catastrophic 1867 crop. Many farmers were in financial trouble, and the Reconstruction process often froze debt proceedings to their benefit. Republicans crafted relief legislation, and most conventions expanded homestead exemptions for this constituency. Bailing out landowners was probably not in the interest of the freedpeople, as black delegates often noted, but political exigency prevailed. Reconstruction's stakeholders were so diverse that it was difficult to keep everyone on board. In northern Georgia, for example, small farmers had been devastated by war, and just as the convention met the courts struck down a stay law. Debtors demanded action to forestall a flood of proceedings, and the delegates barred enforcement of most pre-1865 debts. The new constitution carried with substantial white support, electing the debt relief provision's author, Rufus Bullock, as governor. Congress, however, rejected debt forgiveness outright; the Republican majority insisted the Georgia legislature remove the provision before readmission. It did so, but some up-country Republicans may have taken out their frustration on their black colleagues in the subsequent expulsion vote. Congress defined the outside limits of economic reform, and Republicans elsewhere abandoned the notion. Virginia's Radical constitution, for example, actually barred the legislature from staying the collection of debts.

Beyond the specific provisions, the logistics of constitution-making proved nettlesome. Presidential Reconstruction officials, left provisionally in place over Radical Republican objections, often obstructed the process. North Carolina's governor finely calculated how much he could hinder Reconstruction before the army removed him. Georgia's governor refused to pay for the convention's costs, as provided for under the military Reconstruction acts, and officials fled the state to avoid paying. In addition to these obstacles, the conventions themselves sometimes fell into disarray. Mississippi's delegates once moved outdoors to witness a fistfight between two white members. In Florida moderate and Radical factions formed rival bodies, and the Radicals wrote a constitution draft in a mere three days. Only military pressure forced the predominantly black body to capitulate. Programmatic divisions similarly caused a year's recess in Texas. Given the obstacles, it is surprising that the constitution-writing process proceeded as effectively as it did.

For Reconstruction opponents, a fateful choice loomed. The least disruptive path probably was to ratify the constitutions, secure civil rule and readmittance to Congress, and await a favorable opportunity to vote Republicans out of power. The chances were that white majorities could then curtail voting rights with little interference. Given growing sentiment toward amnesty, a little patience could have avoided much turmoil. Instead most whites rejected even momentary acquiescence to racial equality in favor of resistance. The novelist William Gilmore Simms advised: "Organize promptly in every precinct; get good weapons, establish places of rendezvous, provide signal & pass words; seek your places of rendezvous through the woods & not by the highways, & keep your powder dry." Such private admonitions meant something just as the Klan spread. One can open diaries at random to see sanguinary anticipations of racial conflict.

Orchestrating the chorus of opposition was President Andrew Johnson, who railed against "the effort to Africanize the half of our country." Johnson replaced several army commanders sympathetic to Reconstruction, hoping to forestall completion of the process. Once persuaded that public opinion had turned, he removed Secretary of War Edwin M. Stanton in February 1868. The president was then impeached for violating the terms of the Tenure of Office Act, which protected federal officials from removal without senatorial approval. Whatever the constitutional merit of impeachment on the basis of previous precedent, the motivation was largely Johnson's intervention in the South, and impeachment did stay his hand. The president's acquittal by the Senate in May 1868, by a single vote, was facilitated by assurances to undecided Republican senators that he would desist. While Johnson was thus occupied, the crucial phase of readmission ended, though his acquittal left the army under his control while terrorism spread.

Congressional Reconstruction thus mostly concluded in the spring of 1868. The Military Reconstruction acts had barred voting, temporarily, by former officials who had backed the Confederacy, thus violating their oaths of office. This shouldn't have trimmed the electorate much, perhaps by a few thousand per state, but the congressional terms were nebulous. Large numbers refrained from registration, either out of intimidation or disaffection, as much as a fifth of the white population. The initial registration actually provided African Americans with a majority across the South. Republicans thus had an edge at the polls, but even this was not sufficient everywhere. In the first reconstructed state, Alabama, a white boycott in February 1868 prevented half the electorate from voting, thus apparently frustrating enactment under the Reconstruction acts' terms. Congress quickly modified the law, and events moved ahead. New constitutions won ratification in Arkansas in March; in Louisiana, Georgia, North Carolina, and South Carolina in April; and finally in Florida in May. "The States are jumping into the Union like so many bullfrogs plunging into a pond," a *New York Times* correspondent observed. The majorities were generally large, which demonstrated that in several states Reconstruction won substantial white support. In North Carolina, for example, the vote for the constitution outnumbered black registrants by nearly 14,000, and perhaps a fourth of the white electorate voted for it. In Alabama returns were tabulated by race, and around 7,500 whites braved the boycott. This represented more than a tenth of the registered voters, concentrated in the mountain counties. In South Carolina, on the other hand, the racial polarization was all but complete; a reported 130 whites voted for the constitution in the entire state.

Republicans carried most of the newly created offices, but not everywhere. In Georgia, conservatives and Republican dissidents controlled the new legislature, and they defeated the two Republican-backed candidates for the U.S. Senate. In Louisiana, disaffected Afro-Creoles, asserting racial leadership, nominated an independent Pure Radical ticket and improbably sought conservative support. Most Republicans, however, preferred the Northern newcomer Henry Clay Warmoth, and he won the governorship easily. In Mississippi, ratification miscarried in June 1868. The constitution's disfranchisement provisions re-

portedly galvanized white opposition, and voters rejected ratification outright, encouraged by a spreading Klan campaign. The
Reconstruction process stalled in Virginia as well, due to the military commander's opposition to the Radical constitution.

Still, Reconstruction and its proponents won in most states.
Congress sped the process before it could interfere with the 1868
presidential campaign: a Southern fait accompli seemed safest. In
Alabama, for example, Congress simply disregarded the Democratic boycott and declared substantial compliance, and the state
was readmitted along with five others in June. One might have
assumed that things would now settle down, but the lapse of military authority proved disastrous. Mainstream Republicans,
mindful of Northern sentiment, had preferred a defined end-
point. Therefore once readmission occurred, civil law resumed
and military powers to try offenders disappeared, in the midst of
the Klan upsurge. The failure to convict and remove President
Johnson also discouraged army initiative. General George
Meade, commanding the Department of the South, concluded
that officials should not depend on the military "to settle any tri-
fling difficulty that may occur." In August he ordered troops
withdrawn across the plantation belt, on the grounds of improving discipline. He thought it "better to remove the troops from
the centre of political agitation." Help was a few hours away by
rail, he assured alarmed Republicans, as he headed off to a
Northern vacation.

Thus in the midst of a presidential campaign, civilian rule resumed. In the state capitals the new regimes could operate in relative security, governors could govern and legislators pass laws
with some semblance of normality. But when they returned
home, these same men were in peril of their lives. Alabama's
leading scalawag Radical, D. H. Bingham, was beaten in his
hometown and subsequently died. G. W. Ashburn was killed in
Columbus, Georgia, by dozens of disguised men. Klan notices

proliferated in the Democratic press, bands of night riders operated freely across perhaps half the South. Few Democrats denounced the spreading violence, seeing these measures as the
natural response to the congressional policy. Proscription from
office under the Fourteenth Amendment, ratified that summer,
further antagonized the political elite just as the Klan spread.

Besides, political agitation in the countryside so alarmed
planters that racial extremism looked like prudent self-defense.
One Louisiana sugar planter's diary made this pattern evident. A
Republican rally in New Iberia had whites preparing for a racial
confrontation, as was often the case when rural freedpeople
gathered in town. Whites massed hundreds strong, staying on
alert even after that prospect passed. With Alexandre DeClouet's
involvement, a chapter of the Knights of the White Camelia
formed, and he and family members went "on patrol" for several
nights, whatever precisely that meant. Clearly DeClouet's actions heightened his already strong racial animus. When some
whites recruited black support, he was repulsed, mocking the
"monkeys" in Democratic club uniforms with the concluding ep-
ithet, "Nigger! Nigger! Nigger!!"

The machinery of local government became a particular target. If terrorists could overawe officials, they could disable law
enforcement and then act with impunity. In Appling, Georgia,
Charles Stearns, a failing Northern planter, assumed his position as ordinary judge at the height of the presidential canvass.
Other Republicans took office, but Stearns was beyond the pale;
violence functioned as a sort of white veto over unacceptable officials, and idealists like this former abolitionist often fared
worse than those seen as cynical careerists. When Stearns first
opened his doors, a mob harassed him and some struck him.
"They told me, positively, I could not live, and hold the office to
which I had been elected," he recalled. The sheriff eventually
interrupted, but only to complain about the noise. Attacks esca-

lated, despite the efforts of some to restrain the mob, and a black employee who came to his aid was beaten nearly to death. Stearns had fought slavery in Kansas, but he eventually concluded they would kill him unless he resigned, leaving no one to tell the story.

In areas where blacks predominated, or in upland areas where Unionists were plentiful, Republicans might assume power more smoothly. Even in some of the more closely contested areas, the apparent potential for violence never materialized. Still, it was a chaotic several months, amplified by national events. The impeachment crisis encouraged an apocalyptic mood, and Frank Blair, presidential aspirant and Democratic nominee for vice president, specialized in fierce rhetoric. He denounced Grant as a "mailed warrior" whose bayonets enforced "the domination of an alien race of semi-barbarous men." The incoming president must disperse the carpetbag state governments, by force and extralegally if necessary. Public letters studded with exclamation marks emanated from Blair, persuading Southern Democrats that deliverance was at hand.

Once again outside encouragement lured Southern whites onto treacherous ground. The Northern public, whatever their racial limitations, had not forgotten the war or the possibility of renewed rebellion. Ex-Rebel militancy periodically antagonized them, and terrorist activities were abundantly publicized, most provocatively by the appreciative Southern press. "The Ku-Klux Klan seemed to enjoy reading of their antics in the newspapers," Governor Warmoth recalled. Nathan Bedford Forrest, now the reputed grand dragon, gave an interview in which he reportedly boasted: "There is not a radical leader in this town but is a marked man; and if a trouble should break out, not one of them would be left alive." Forced to explain such statements, Democratic newspapers simultaneously denied the Klan's existence, or argued that it was all pranksterism, or contended that the individual victims deserved their fate. The hash of inconsistent denials all but proved the prevalence of terrorism.

The Democratic ticket compounded the problem. The contrast between Democrat Horatio Seymour, a wartime critic of the Lincoln administration, and the Republican candidate U. S. Grant needed little explanation. General Grant himself won nomination over Radical misgivings, and he gave a solid impression of nonideological leadership, reinforced by his judicious acceptance statement urging, "Let Us Have Peace." With Congressional Reconstruction largely complete, most Northerners concluded to let well enough alone rather than commence the process yet again. Grant carried the electoral college easily, but he won only 52.7 percent of the popular vote, which suggests how closely the electorate was divided. The terrorist issue probably determined the outcome in the crucial Northern states.

In the South the Klan mobilization suppressed Republican vote totals drastically in two states. In Georgia, Grant received no votes in three black majority counties, and in one county the Republican count fell from 1,222 to a single vote. Louisiana's Republican vote similarly dropped from 69,000 in April to 33,000 in November. Elsewhere Democrats, sensing defeat, stayed away from the polls, and Grant carried the other readmitted states, with still unreconstructed Mississippi, Virginia, and Texas passing the season in relative peace. After defeat the political scene looked entirely different. Southern whites had assumed the North must return to its senses and sweep the nightmare away. Instead Republicans won majorities in Congress, buttressed by a host of new Southern representatives, and Grant would be president for four years, perhaps eight. Yet again, some reflected, Democratic extremism had led to disaster.

The political failure of the terrorist campaign deserves emphasis. Nowhere did the Klan drive the new governments from power. Violence infuriated state leaders without actually disabling them. Republicans would be able to tax and spend and rewrite the laws, and now they would assume local office even in the restive rural areas. It was a frightening mixture from the point of view of those who still had substantial property to protect; small wonder that wealthy men now began making conciliatory gestures. The Republicans assuming power were simultaneously resentful, exuberant at their own confirmation in power and desperate to reconfigure the region.

5

Railroads, Development, and Reconstructing Society

HAVING IMPLEMENTED black suffrage, created new constitutions, and survived the resulting hurricane, Southern Republicans finally experienced an interlude of relative calm. The national victory of U. S. Grant and the Republicans confirmed Congressional Reconstruction. A sympathetic federal government would ensure the completion of the process in the three remaining unreconstructed states—Mississippi, Texas, and Virginia. Everywhere but Virginia, elected Republicans won formal control and exercised it for some years. But how would Republicans make the changes they sought permanent? Translating momentary state power into lasting transformation was the task.

Momentary is the crucial point. The overthrow of ten existing state governments and the imposition of equal suffrage infuriated most of the white population. Seldom have so large a number of citizens in a democracy been so antagonized by those in power. Radical Reconstruction violated all their sense of social order and constitutional governance; random correspondence is scattered with diatribes. Thus Radical Reconstruction's implementation often left its proponents in an extraordinary situation, governing a hostile majority through the forms of civil law. In retrospect the prospects for a positive outcome through the electoral process seem slim, given the size, wealth, and resources of the Southern opposition. And, as one North Carolinian warned, "if we ever get beat we are gone and Trampled under foot." Southern Republican leaders necessarily had to fish in troubled waters, to change the underlying electoral balance drastically.

The Republican administrations could not survive without outside protection. Governor Brownlow thought that without army backing his legislature "would be broken up *by a mob in forty-eight hours*." Support by Washington, in turn, depended on the commitment of Northern Republicans, and on the party's ability to maintain a national majority. Radical sentiment owed much to the passions of the moment, and given underlying Northern racial attitudes, Southern Republicans could not count on protection forever. Republicans needed to convert a spasmodic congressional grant of equal suffrage into permanent change. Disfranchisement of former Confederates had temporarily given Republicans an edge at the polls, but the new constitutions provided for few limitations on suffrage, and even these were soon abandoned. The national electorate had demonstrated growing resistance to such measures, and Southern Republicans could not afford to antagonize Northern sentiment.

Only two states had substantial black majorities. Without disfranchisement of some ex-Confederates, Republicans were a prospective minority most everywhere else. Beyond this, it was unlikely that Northern sentiment would indefinitely sanction governments based primarily on black ballots, and negative "carpetbagger" imagery spread surprisingly quickly. To be seen as legitimate with the all-important Northern public, Republicans needed a respectable white following. *Harper's Weekly* spoke enthusiastically of the notion that "the real work of reconstruction at the South must be done by native or long-resident Southern white men." For incoming Republican officeholders, this meant outreach to the native white majority. Civil rights, of course, had no positive appeal to them. At best one might find a pragmatic sense among some planters that getting along with their labor force might be helpful. Wartime loyalties were little better as a political emphasis, given that the mass of whites had yielded allegiance to the Davis government. Most of the electorate was composed of Confederate veterans bonded through common travail. An Unconditional Unionist minority existed, but they were already numbered among Republican voters. Militant Unionists were hated as lawless renegades, and emphasizing their cause would win few new recruits.

There were, however, Democratic liabilities that persisted, especially a lingering wariness of states' rights ideologues. For many "Conservatives"—mostly defined as those who had supported Bell or Douglas in 1860—political behavior during the secession crisis remained a live issue. Elitist by temperament and recent experience, former Whigs and Conservatives instead wanted to emphasize economic recovery and solicit Northern investment rather than engage in sectional conflict. For those with substantial economic interests to protect, the fruits of Democratic leadership had not been reassuring. Hard-liners had arrayed the white population behind outright resistance, but Grant's victory sobered many. Continued alliance with the Northern Democratic minority looked counterproductive, and Conservative delegations began meeting with the president-elect, promising goodwill. Some now depicted themselves as a political third force. Mitigating Republican rule seemed a reasonable interim tactic, and for professional politicians, dependent on office for a living, it offered personal opportunities. Even Confederate generals like James Longstreet sought office under the Grant administration. Lewis Parsons, previously Alabama's provisional governor, had been a bitter opponent of concessions, but he turned a new leaf. So did ex-governors James Orr of South Carolina and Robert Patton of Alabama. Such men had been recently proclaiming their racist bona fides, but the Grant administration, with its affinity for wealth and station, proved receptive to such recruits.

Individual conversions hardly represented a popular groundswell, but they did suggest that inroads were possible. Still, Republicans needed a tangible appeal, something that could overshadow civil rights, wartime loyalty, and other less popular issues. They needed to focus people on the future. Public education was certainly one theme, tied to national notions of progress. Enlightened whites might endorse the concept, and those who hoped for schooling for their own children, but it had only limited appeal. Albion Tourgée later observed, "They are not over fond of education here at the best. Our poor white population have to be fed a heap of soft corn to take much stock in it. . . ." Expanded schools suggested taxing white property holders to aid poor blacks, which is not the message Republicans sought.

Republicans wanted to enlist some white voters' economic self-interest strongly. A modest number could tip the electoral balance, and any effective appeal would reduce animosity. Given how economically pressed most Unionists were, Republicans certainly sought measures to benefit whites of modest means. They expanded homestead exemptions on proceedings for debt. Republicans sometimes backed more drastic debt relief, as in the Georgia constitution. At election times Republicans regularly broadcast class-based appeals. These measures, however, had only limited effect on the mass of farmers, whose wartime and racial loyalties were nearly impervious to economic arguments— at least under the auspices of the hated Republican party. There was also the problem of how such appeals resonated with the all-important national public. Northern journals of opinion like *The Nation* pilloried redistributive policies as communistic. Even on crucial matters like the currency and credit scarcity that hurt farmers nationwide, President Grant and Eastern Republicans thought sound money the highest priority.

Congress made these pro-business priorities clear. Even at the height of Radical Republican influence, the wartime vogue of confiscation dissipated. Thaddeus Stevens's land confiscation proposals lost overwhelmingly in the House. Congress enacted a federal bankruptcy overhaul, and one might have expected that Republicans would seek the breakup of the large plantations. Instead they expedited a fresh start by Southern debtors, thus helping stabilize the social structure, as a recent study has observed. Similarly, before the war numerous railroads received land grants on the condition of completion within a number of years. Some Southern Radicals wanted to distribute the now technically forfeited land to homesteaders. Thaddeus Stevens pushed such a proposal, but the Senate instead reconfirmed the grants.

At the national level the Republicans were the party of economic growth. If Southern Republicans were to craft an economic appeal, it could not depend on Northern inattention. Major initiatives had to be consistent with the administration's solicitude for corporate enterprise. Even the Grant administration's reform-minded Republican critics opposed appeals to working-class and agrarian interests. In this constrained context, state sponsorship of economic development became the panacea. Modernization was part of the whole Yankee package of social progress, and Northerners were strongly represented in the Republican leadership. Besides, many white Southerners welcomed economic diversification. Former governor Orr observed, "I am tired of South Carolina as she was. . . . I would have her acres teem with life and vigor and intelligence, as do those of Massachusetts." One conservative, Alexander H. H. Stuart, pointed out that Virginians could not reverse the national election or black suffrage: "Let these [political] questions be settled—it matters not how—and population and capital will flow [in] . . . building up our cities, opening our mines, buying and improving our land, constructing new railways and canals, and giving vigor and activity to our industrial interests." Continued intransigence would only deter investors.

Talk of an industrial New South would become common in the 1880s under different auspices, but the idea had long held appeal. As one Florida woman crisply observed, "Feebleness of purpose won't do in these days of Yankee goaheadativeness." It made emotional sense to concentrate on matters within control, and the evident vogue of Northern commercial values offered Reconstruction supporters an entree. Republicans pursued a number of options, from levee construction to subsidizing factories, but railroads were the obvious priority. War had mangled the South's transportation system while the rest of the nation raced ahead with state and federal aid. Starting with the transcontinental railroad, Congress had bestowed more than 100 million Western acres and large loans upon railroad companies. It was a fateful coincidence that Reconstruction occurred alongside the national railroad mania, which would deflate at an inopportune time. Still, if Reconstruction supporters sought social transformation, railroad measures seemed promising. The *New York Times* hailed the Southern commercial and railroad renaissance as the best possible sign.

Railroad promotion appealed precisely to those elements of the Southern opposition most inclined to collaboration, the former Whigs and their Conservative successors. Before its demise in the early 1850s, economic development was the Whig party's core emphasis. Subsidy measures gained bipartisan support during the prewar boom, and railroad expansion was dramatic. The Civil War spread devastation, but afterward Presidential Reconstruction often placed Conservative proponents of aid in office. Furthermore, as planters made the transition from slaveholding "laborlords" to landlords, infrastructure investment became more attractive.

Even so, the South's poverty and anomalous legal status deterred outside investment. In 1866 all the ex-Confederate states together added less railroad mileage than Pennsylvania. From 1865 to 1868, Mississippi and Louisiana laid no track at all, and Arkansas and Florida nearly none. During Presidential Reconstruction, Southern states often found it impossible to renegotiate existing debts, much less fund new subsidy measures, though several recklessly tried. Alabama actually passed a general aid program while Congress debated Military Reconstruction. Unfortunately, as one broker observed, bonds sold only to bargain hunters exploiting chaos. It was a frustrating logjam, especially for leaders with entrepreneurial interests. Conservatives hardly welcomed black suffrage, but it held a silver lining. Once the Reconstruction process was completed, state financing of railroads again became possible.

During the implementation stage of Radical Reconstruction, little could be done. The constitutional conventions were hardly conducive to financial measures, though North Carolina's approved large grants anyway. Elsewhere delegates generally satisfied themselves with endorsing aid in principle. As Congress readmitted the Southern states beginning in mid-1868, bond prices generally improved. The availability of outside capital, much of it from Europe, encouraged a flood of promotion measures in 1869 and 1870, the high point of Republican rule. Governor William W. Holden of North Carolina explained the rationale. Sounding a bit Hamiltonian, his inaugural address observed that a public debt could be a source of stability. Extending transportation would "stimulate agriculture and the mechanic arts, build up our sea ports . . . draw thither immigrants from the Northern States and from Europe . . . [and] give employment to thousands of our people. . . ." In Holden's state, white Republican support was most substantial in the transportation-starved West, which encouraged expensive projects through the mountains.

The features of the railroad program were reasonably consistent. Republican legislatures freely granted liberal corporate charters. Several states simply awarded state bonds to companies as a direct subsidy. Arkansas and especially Alabama approved general aid laws rather than approving projects piecemeal. Subsidy laws often provided that as a company completed track, the state would guarantee its bonds to help sell them. Texas pledged $10,000 a mile, Georgia $15,000, and North Carolina up to $20,000. If the railroad was completed and prospered, the bonds would be paid, and the cost for taxpayers would be nothing. States had the right to sell off the line to get their investment back. Since building the railroads cost considerably more than the endorsements, the policy seemed safe enough. Most laws as written were not obviously flawed, and they contained numerous provisions that should have protected the public interest.

Some states went beyond these safeguards. The Texas constitution prohibited land grants, though the provision was later removed at Democratic initiative. Republican Governor Edmund Davis opposed aid measures, vetoing several. His Radical following helped defeat override attempts, and the Texas state debt remained modest. Mississippi was still more cautious, escaping all embarrassment. Decades before, Mississippi had defaulted on its bonds, and the constitution ratified in 1869 prohibited the loan of state credit, though later Republican legislatures finessed the ban. Even enactment of a subsidy program did not necessarily mean ruin. Arkansas carefully settled overdue and disputed state bonds before proceeding. It established a state board to approve individual grants, and only four roads actually received state money. According to the historian Mark Summers, the Arkansas program avoided financial injury while railroad track grew from 86 to 490 miles.

The larger point is that the aid program had some success. In 1868 the states undergoing Reconstruction had 8,400 miles of railroad, but by the end of 1871 that figure grew to more than 11,000. This represented an increase of 31 percent, with most of the growth in the Republican-governed states. After the war Tennessee alone added more than 300 miles, and a later Democratic governor observed that "no intelligent man can regret the policy which inaugurated the system. . . ." Much of the region's growth, moreover, would occur in the piedmont and mountains. In time these railroads indeed helped bring the cotton mills and heavy industry that transformed the upland economy.

In retrospect it is easy to conclude that the railroad program was a mistake. Republican leaders opened a Pandora's box of corporate abuse. Still, Congress had given them a fragile lease on power, and in this desperate context it is difficult to fault the political logic. They could hardly go to a predominantly ex-Confederate electorate solely as the party of Union and racial equality. Republicans needed to take risks, to offer a positive and inclusive vision. Moreover the aid program was initially popular among the white population: in Arkansas a statewide referendum on the aid law passed almost five to one. Ex-Confederate generals were conspicuous as company presidents, and Jefferson Davis himself fielded job offers. Few in the commercial elite cautioned against aid as a general policy. Democrats only occasionally suggested these initiatives should wait, on the grounds that Reconstruction governments were too irresponsible to trust with them. Given such enthusiasm, as Summers concluded, "the Republicans would have been fools not to have turned it to their use, and lunatics to oppose it."

The Democratic press lauded the railroad policy, primarily concerned that their own communities would be bypassed, and local measures often sailed through with little opposition. Partisan lines dissolved on such issues. For example, the *Tuscaloosa Monitor* was unsurpassed in its enthusiasm for the Ku Klux Klan, with its editor masterminding terrorist raids. Still, when the Republican-connected builders of the Alabama & Chattanooga line arrived, these stereotypic Boston interlopers got a warm press reception. "Hail to the Stantons, who are not carpetbaggers," the paper proclaimed. To their energies Tuscaloosa owed its present prosperity. Reports of legislative bribery were widespread, but the *Monitor* praised these entrepreneurs to the skies as public benefactors.

Democratic leaders and editors frequently had railroad connections themselves, and subsidies won bipartisan support in the legislatures. Still, it was the one Republican-identified policy enjoying widespread support. As Governor Holden observed in November 1868, "The people of [North Carolina] are so fully committed to internal improvements that I deem it necessary to say but little on the subject." Republicans sometimes enacted such policies without black aid; Tennessee's Unionist government initiated an ambitious program before black suffrage. While Republicans generally favored aid, the specific role of the freedpeople has received less attention. Perhaps because older scholarship blamed equal suffrage for whatever went amiss, more modern scholars shied away from the topic. But African Americans had a lot riding on these initiatives, and their role needs explanation.

It is admittedly difficult to discern a singular African-American perspective on the fateful railroad program. There were few rallies, petitions, and the like from constituents. Spokesmen seldom addressed the issue until it became a major liability. Frederick Douglass occasionally backed railroad aid in his *New National Era*, but more as a party measure than as a priority. Civil rights, terrorism, and partisan loyalty to the Republicans—these were the issues that counted. The *New Orleans Tribune* warned legislators, "Before all matters of general interest, it becomes the colored members of the Assembly to see that the rights of those whom they particularly represent, are acknowledged and guaranteed." Railroads were well down the list of priorities, involving financial matters upon which voters had little direct experience. The reality, as Democrats pointed out endlessly, was that if property taxes were raised, few freedpeople would feel it directly. For black leaders, this made the issue subject to tactical considerations. Constituent demands were so urgent on everything else that here expediency could prevail.

Railroad promotion promised attractive benefits. Construction provided short-term jobs, always an urgent matter for working people seeking cash in slack seasons. In mid-1869 one railroad executive complained that projects were bidding up construction labor, indicating a positive short-term impact for unskilled employees. One press account claimed there were fourteen thousand construction jobs in mid-1870 in Alabama alone. If the railroads were completed, and the promised industrial development ensued, it would provide a needed alternative to plantation work. Moreover state endorsement of railroad company bonds did not necessarily cut into state revenues needed for schools and social services. Although failure might have drastic consequences, the possibility seemed remote. The financial community generally thought these measures were safe. Black leaders seldom had the experience to make them doubt the prevailing wisdom.

Here, then, was a welcome chance for black politicians to identify themselves with the material interests of their communities. A show of bipartisanship could win plaudits in unaccustomed quarters, or at least halt the drumbeat of press abuse. At a time of widespread terrorist assassination, this was no small attraction. Besides, the railroad companies sometimes placed Republican politicians on their boards of directors and hired black speakers. The Mississippi legislator Robert Gleed undertook speaking engagements in support of a regional project. While this was presumably a paying proposition, it also served as an unaccustomed gesture of respect by opposition whites. Such racial recognition probably loomed large in leaders' minds.

At the local level, grassroots influence was more direct. Reconstruction generated a host of local aid measures. Development efforts sometimes featured referenda on public endorsement; in Mississippi, for example, county subsidies required a two-thirds popular vote, and in Alabama a simple majority. Within counties, black suffrage shifted the distribution of voters in favor of plantation neighborhoods. In local campaigns the contending factions frequently competed for black support, calling public rallies for their benefit. Violence seldom disrupted these elections, even during the Klan heyday. Freedpeople thus got the unusual chance to vote in relative safety, to weigh in alongside their fellow citizens on the railroads as a nonpartisan matter of importance. This may well have seemed more important than the issue's merits. Moreover the pattern of support was generally geographic, based on the route a line would take. Since railroads often ran through wealthy plantation districts, freedmen often lined up with Whiggish planters, precisely the whites least prone to espouse terrorist violence.

One might view railroad subsidies as an indirect anti-Klan measure since terrorist activities were most persistent away from the rail lines. Subsidies might also buy off discontent, as none other than the notorious Nathan Bedford Forrest demonstrated. In early 1868 the former general orchestrated the Klan's spread from his home in Memphis and during his business travels. But when Forrest became president of a railroad project his partisan tone changed. Soon he called for the Klan to disband, and he traveled up and down the cotton belt promoting his railroad company, lobbying (and perhaps bribing) elected officials. Forrest concluded that "railroads had no part of politics" and that he "wanted the assistance of everybody." In one instance he urged terrorists to leave a Republican officeholder alone and assisted his eventual escape. In 1871 Forrest claimed to have some four hundred black employees working for him. He called on black voters to endorse his railroad, and he spoke appreciatively of their willingness to do so. His behavior is susceptible to various interpretations, but it suggests that black voters overlooked Forrest's past misdeeds in the face of local needs and his current behavior.

One can scarcely fault the freedpeople or their leaders for supporting subsidy measures. The policy turned out badly, but nothing else held hope of placating the opposition without compromising civil rights or social spending. The issue of *how* Republican leaders implemented subsidies is another matter. Modern revisionist historians generally don't emphasize how problematic Reconstruction financial management often was. Model behavior by officials was unlikely, this being the national high point of corruption, but it was Reconstruction's best hope. As Horace Greeley's *Tribune* intoned, honest government was "imperative, on many accounts" in the Southern states. Radical Republicans in the North were an earnest lot, social reformers and Protestant churchpeople, and nothing could sully their commitment more quickly than peculation. Nor did Republican businessmen appreciate financial chicanery. Freedpeople were uniquely vulnerable to anything that imperiled their moral authority. Whatever went wrong, black voters were likely to get blamed, given all the racial stereotypes in play. African-American leaders were not the main actors, or the major beneficiaries in corruption, but then they didn't need to be. Even behaving like their Gilded Age peers would do immense harm.

Some Republican leaders became aware of the corruption problem early. Late in 1868, U.S. Senator John Pool warned of the rumors he had heard about North Carolina. He warned that some Republicans were "putting in jeopardy the interests of the State & life of our party, for their private, pecuniary gains." Pool expressed incredulity that so many seemed blind to the risk. These problems were compounded by fiscal irresponsibility. During Presidential Reconstruction the state had not paid full interest on its existing debt for years. Ex-governor Jonathan Worth, who enjoyed the Republicans' financial incompetence, gleefully pointed out the implication of the large expenditures: "No debtor who promises to pay a dollar for fifty cents, intends to pay."

The constitutional convention in North Carolina authorized millions for Western railroads, and the first Reconstruction legislature approved still more in direct aid. A *New York Times* correspondent observed that petitions poured in from all over the state. He noted that no provision had yet been made for schools, which suggests how little the black minority determined the priorities. Unfortunately lawmakers balked at raising taxes, on the assumption that escalating land values should pay the interest painlessly. A subsequent dispute over the legality of some of the bonds spooked Wall Street. Unable to borrow a modest sum, the state defaulted on its interest payments six months into Republican rule. The state then authorized yet more grants to bail out the imperiled lines. By 1870, as Governor Holden admitted, the failing companies dumped their bonds for "small sums" fruitlessly. The state accumulated a thirty-million-dollar debt, with little to show.

North Carolina's swift meltdown was unique. Elsewhere the aid program initially helped the Republicans. One Democratic politician complained that the "unscrupulous men [who] have charge of our R. Rs. will give free tickets to the scalawag orators, domestic and foreign." Partisan bitterness also encouraged indifference toward taxpayers. In South Carolina, Governor Robert Scott believed that extravagant expenditures by the legislature occurred "in retaliation" for Klan violence. All the talk of the benign effect of property taxation likewise encouraged spending.

For newcomers like Scott, there was also an apparent personal dimension. These measures opened avenues to respectable society. Then again, Governor Scott's own railroad investments also encouraged his enthusiasm for subsidies.

The bond measures provided short-term potential benefits, and the economic omens looked favorable. The price of cotton improved in early 1868, staying relatively strong in 1869 and most of 1870. Jefferson Davis himself observed that the South enjoyed two years of improving material prosperity. Labor relations stabilized as tenant farming spread. Especially after the tumultuous presidential campaign ended, planters turned their attention toward making money. In 1868 Southern state bonds approached par value in some cases. Guaranteed company bonds sold well too, and as even ex-governor Worth conceded, "the enormous expenditures on the R. Rs. etc. produce some enterprise in the localities where the expenditures are made." Land prices near the proposed lines soared, 50 percent or more. Georgia's government claimed that land values along the ten subsidized lines increased more than the value of the endorsements.

Railroads shifted the structure of trade away from the antebellum pattern of river-based commerce. Planters dealt directly with Eastern markets and merchandized goods to their tenants at plantation stores. In the highlands, farmers could get staple crops to market and procure fertilizer, moving from self-sufficiency in food to participation in the cash economy. Stores with names like New York Clothing Boutique began advertising in places like Tuscaloosa, and fresh paint was much in demand. Urban dreams proliferated. Birmingham didn't even exist before the war, but coal and iron made this rail crossing into the New South's powerhouse of heavy industry. When the British correspondent Robert Somers started on his tour of the South in 1870, he could hardly miss the impact. Okalona, Mississippi, had been all but destroyed in the war, but now it was a town of several thousand, with a long street of brick stores and offshoots built toward the railway depot. Likewise in Meridian, railroad construction brought "labour, money, and traffic about the little town," propelling its initial stages of growth. Soon it too boasted brick warehouses and a row of stores. Social dislocation ensued, as a bloody riot would soon reveal, but the economic changes still looked welcome.

For all these benefits, practical problems proliferated. Legislators passed numerous projects simultaneously, for geographic balance and maximum political support. Subsidies encouraged thinly capitalized projects, which induced hard-pressed managers to evade legal protections. Aid laws also enticed local elites to begin projects with minimal capital, knowing that if they could build a few miles they might secure sufficient subsidies to continue. These factors resulted in eye-popping if somewhat hypothetical debts for prospective contingent liabilities—that is, obligations for lines that had first to be built and then go bankrupt to cost taxpayers anything. Alabama's prewar debt was under $6 million, but it would soar to a contingent debt of more than $30 million. Louisiana's potential liability reached $41 million, though the effective figure was more like $25 million. Several other states had much smaller debts, but unfortunately for the Republicans these received less attention. The undoubted reality was bracing enough. Several Southern states doubled their bonded debt, and economic development rather than, say, schools comprised the bulk.

The most destructive bond episode occurred in South Carolina, where high officials behaved recklessly. The state was already in default on paying interest, but the new government expanded social spending and also funded a railroad project across the western mountains. Unfortunately tax revenues fell massively below expectations. Governor Scott later explained, "Without a system of taxation that could be made available, without credit in the money markets, [and] her bonds selling at 25c on the dollar," only drastic measures could forestall "complete anarchy." State officials printed bonds, some apparently without legislative authority, borrowing against them to fund government operations. The *New York Tribune* reported that bonds were sent to a financial agent who, "instead of selling them, pledged them for loans, and so went on pledging and borrowing like clock-work—the securities all the while falling in value, and being occasionally sold by alarmed lenders."

South Carolina officials manipulated bond prices through purchases with borrowed money. Worse, the secretive maneuvers let the state treasurer appropriate some proceeds—for which he was later convicted. Governor Scott, the treasurer, and the financial agent all accused one another of theft, and this largely played out in New York before the national press. The Republican legislature disavowed many of the bonds, leaving the state's credit ruined. Other states had similar problems on a lesser scale. Governor Harrison Reed repeatedly faced impeachment, but his own explanation of what happened to $4 million in Florida bonds is unsettling enough: "It appears that the bonds were intrusted by the [endorsed] company to one of the firms of swindlers who abound in New York, which, by fraud and villainy, they have diverted much of the proceeds. . . ." The money to construct the railroad was gone.

Southern woes dovetailed with revelations of railroad chicanery across the country. Numerous ways were found to turn public subsidies to private account. Government endorsements could be used to enrich contracting firms, which were themselves often owned by the railroad directors; this would be the basis of the notorious Credit Mobilier scheme, in which congressmen were offered access to stock assured of rapid growth. By mid-1870 even the *New York Times* was editorializing against the whole policy of state and local aid. *The Nation* observed that

"The popular feeling in regard to municipal aid to railroad construction is running as thoughtlessly in one direction now as it did in the other a few years ago. At present, the tendency is to cut the system up root and branch, just as not long ago it was to subsidize everything." In this mood, emerging Reconstruction problems encountered little patience. Public watchdog Charles Francis Adams, Jr., dismissed Southern railroad bond transactions as not worth the trouble of exposure.

Under Reconstruction's confused circumstances, individual leaders largely determined how the aid programs turned out. Where they were not personally implicated or politically beholden to the railroads, it made tremendous difference. Governors Alcorn and Ames in Mississippi and Davis in Texas, for example, vetoed numerous bills and kept debt down. Alabama's Governor William H. Smith, on the other hand, exemplified everything that could go wrong. He was on the board of one endorsed railroad along with several moderate Republican allies. Despite widespread reports of bribery for a $2 million loan to complete the Alabama & Chattanooga and other roads, Governor Smith signed the legislation. By his own admission he also signed nearly $600,000 in unauthorized company bonds. The governor's office didn't feel authorized to keep track, and, incredibly, told the company so. After a certain point projects became too big to allow them to fail. Governor Smith's Democratic successor discovered this when the unfinished railroad defaulted and he refused to honor the state guarantee, pending an investigation. This upright course of action undermined nearly all the other state-endorsed projects.

Irresponsible behavior by Republican officials, much of it clandestine and virtually all by whites, imperiled the reputation of their African-American constituency. It also encouraged the legislative bribery that became the epitome of Reconstruction's woes. It is difficult to separate fact from legend, but passage of subsidies was often characterized by malfeasance. Promoters willing to resort to open bribery could generally find legislative collaborators. Democrats generally participated, but Republican majorities naturally received the blame. Several elements played into this pattern of behavior, sheer poverty being among them. At the Florida constitutional convention, one Radical observed of his faction "nearly all of our delegates are poor. Probably 3/4 of them have to borrow money to come with. . . ." Similarly in Louisiana, one resolution observed that "Many Members of this Convention are without money, and are depending upon their [pay] warrants in order to get means. . . ." When rural legislators ran short of funds away from home, they had limited options. Too, lawmakers often had little experience in dealing with corporate blandishments, and there was great turnover in the legislatures. A combination of camaraderie and partisan loyalty excused dubious behavior, especially on matters secondary to constituents. Inexperienced lawmakers betrayed little awareness that their supporters' interests were being imperiled. The problem was that corporate favors needed to be passed only once while Republican voters needed an intact reputation.

The issue inevitably took on a racial hue. The Northern reporter Edward King somehow blamed "the great mass of densely ignorant and ambitious blacks" for North Carolina's fiscal ruin, mistakenly calling them a majority of the state's residents. Such sloppy characterizations were misleading; those dispensing bribes were white railroad officials, generally Democrats. For all the talk of corrupt blacks and carpetbaggers, there is no discernible pattern of black-dominated Radical factions taking the initiative on railroad issues. There are, however, several examples of Northern newcomers, like South Carolina's Governor Scott and his associates, being personally involved in railroads receiving aid. Several flamboyant Northern promoters also resorted to outright bribery, which when revealed tainted everyone. The most notorious example, perhaps, is General Milton Littlefield, who received aid from North Carolina and then spent the proceeds in Florida, to qualify for further subsidies there. Politicians were damaged by their association with Republican-connected railroad promoters, the term "carpetbagger" being freely applied to both.

When problems arose it proved easy to shift responsibility onto black colleagues. Louisiana's Governor Warmoth, himself ethically challenged, nonetheless blamed the "great many men in our legislature who are ignorant of the manipulations of lobbyists." Since many were only recently enfranchised they had "to be nursed." Given the shadowy transactions, it was difficult for those at a distance to evaluate these self-serving claims. Legislators taking and dispersing large sums were preponderantly white, as the initial composition of committee chairs and Republican leadership would suggest. The pattern inclined black legislators to follow suit, in a cockeyed quest for racial parity. In Florida, for example, one black legislator recalled that his colleagues formed a sort of shakedown caucus to ensure that they received a cut of the largesse. South Carolina's Beverly Nash explained such thinking: "I was supporting these [railroad] Bills because I thought . . . it was right, and I merely took the money because I thought I might as well have it and invest it here as for them to carry it off out of State." But pocketing cash inevitably had political consequences when exposed. This was "How to Put South Carolina into the Hands of the Former Slaveholders," as Frederick Douglass's newspaper warned.

Such behavior seems to have been common. In Virginia a handwritten memoir by George Teamoh claimed that the other five black legislators all accepted money for a railroad measure. The ex-slave rebuffed a company agent who came to his quarters bearing thousands of dollars. Alabama's Representative Jere Haralson provides a vivid sense of the legislative context. The previously mentioned Alabama & Chattanooga aid measure loosened large sums from the Stanton brothers and other firms, reportedly tens of thousands to one scalawag committee chair alone. Haralson heard many such rumors, and his black colleagues groused about their paltry share. Haralson went to company officials' hotel rooms for a chat, but he had to go to some lengths to get his "loan." A complex mixture of motivations seems evident. Haralson heard the railroad men argue that it was an important road and financially sound, suggesting actual consideration of the merits. It was seen as a party measure, and his fifty dollars looks more like a tip than a serious bribe. Money changed hands freely, but this frank account also suggests the peripheral involvement of African-American lawmakers in the outcome.

Haralson's description reveals something else. His candor suggests that he didn't expect the episode to hurt his political future, and he was indeed elected to Congress. This former slave revealed himself as an articulate, and witty, defender of his constituents' viewpoint. Exposure of representatives' misdeeds, especially by critics pursuing a white supremacist agenda, would elicit a conflicted response: private regret and embarrassment, but also solidarity. Freedpeople distrusted the taxpayer complaints, rightly believing them to have ulterior motives. Republican officeholders were shielded by the reality that, ultimately, the issue was secondary to their constituents. As Congressman John Roy Lynch would later observe, "It matters little to the colored race in the South about the dishonesty of leaders, for if the Republican governments had stolen money, the Democrats proposed to steal rights." What Republicans said and did openly on racial justice issues mattered more than what they did surreptitiously on financial ones. Given the ruinous consequences of Democratic victory, it is difficult to fault their priorities.

But Northern opinion responded differently: *Harper's Weekly* took Lynch to task for his candid statement, cluelessly suggesting the freedmen's fate was safer in the hands of honest Democrats. By the early 1870s even formerly Radical editors deplored the misdeeds of the Reconstruction governments. Whitelaw Reid of the *New York Tribune* privately disavowed the idea that "a minority composed of negroes and disreputable carpetbaggers can permanently and safely govern a large majority in any American state." His associate, Horace Greeley, was America's leading Radical journalist, but he returned from the South in mid-1871 denouncing carpetbaggers: "They went to issuing State bonds. They pretended to use them in aid of railroads and other improvements. But the improvements were not made, and the bonds stuck in the issuers' pockets." Similarly the influential *Nation*, despite its onetime Radical origins, denounced shamelessly corrupt governments that victimized "nearly every Southern State." It wasn't true, but the editors actually regretted that Klan misdeeds might distract the public from this more important concern.

Even Radical Republican politicians began talking this way, people whose egalitarian principles would seem beyond reproach. Senator Charles Sumner was the national figure most devoted to racial equality, but President Grant's administration antagonized him. In 1871 Sumner warned blacks that thieves and moneylenders must be driven from the temple, and he soon referred to scandals in the federal service as robberies. In September 1872 he deplored the disordered finances of the Southern states. He hoped that Southern whites might finally accept black suffrage, because as things stood they were "sinking under the intolerable burden" of corruption. Sumner's rhetoric increasingly resembled that of Reconstruction's opponents. "So colossal has been the scale of plunder that even authentic report seems like fable," he concluded.

South Carolina, with its large black majority, epitomized Reconstruction's ills, and Northern correspondents became the vehicle of exposure. Reporters once had trekked southward to critique ex-Rebel misdeeds, but now they paraded their own second thoughts on racial matters. Once denunciation of carpetbaggers became routine, criticism of their black supporters became easier. James S. Pike's *The Prostrate State: South Carolina under Negro Government* (1873) was the most influential of the exposés. Having an anti-slavery background, Pike was perfectly situated to make the case that "so universally implicated is everybody about the government" that malfeasance ran riot. His harsh conclusion was that "The civilized and educated white race was under foot, prostrate and powerless, and the black barbarian reigned in its stead." This emphasis turned easily to outright racism, and one could multiply such statements endlessly.

Democrats had been saying this sort of thing for years, but now more Northerners began to believe it. Why? To some extent the popularity of Radical Republicanism had grown out of wartime patriotism. With the lapse of time, the anger at white Southerners was likely to recede. New issues were moving to the fore, issues involving public and corporate malfeasance rather than slavery and its evils. Republicans initiated the Southern railroad program in a national climate of awareness of governmental corruption. The political fortunes of President Grant contributed to this. With official and corporate abuse in the spotlight, an expansive national government that could protect Southern freedmen's civil rights looked less appealing. The railroad program had much to do with how this climate of opinion developed on racial matters, especially in the crucial Northern states. It set the stage for abandonment when the economy crashed, taking nearly all the endorsed railroads and governments that aided them into bankruptcy.

6

Race, Faction, and Grant

THE RAILROAD WOES may have been avoidable in theory, but in practice it is difficult to imagine Republican leaders pursuing alternate policies. The factional troubles that beset Reconstruction seem equally inescapable. Southern Republicans were prone to internal divisions, both over policy and patronage matters, which undermined their repute before the national public. But given the issues, and the political culture in which they operated, it is difficult to imagine things working out differently. Nearly everywhere factional meltdowns characterized Republican rule, which must say something about the Reconstruction process itself. The disparate composition of the coalition bred internal strife, and the striking thing is how well freedpeople fared for years in these contests.

The basic problem is obvious: African Americans were a minority of the region's voters, and they could not rule unaided. A relatively small number of receptive whites held electoral leverage. Especially at first, the whites most drawn to the Republicans were wartime Unionists and draft resisters. Early alliance with these insurgents tied African Americans to a political agenda based on Radical disfranchisement and proscription of ex-Confederates. As these measures became less viable, civil rights itself defined Republican factional divisions, and the instability of the Reconstruction coalition became more apparent.

Because native white Republicans were so diverse, the category "scalawag" is misleading in all respects save one: few thought racial justice a priority. Rooted as they were in their communities, they were reluctant to flout racial convention more than their politics required. When individual leaders did so, they lost credibility with their less personally invested Unionist following. Scalawags therefore drew an emphatic line between civil equality, which they might support with suitable qualifications, and social equality, which they generally disavowed. That distinction was more easily made in theory than in practice, and articulating it wore on their black allies' nerves.

Scalawags were shaped by the mental legacy of slavery, and their racial attitudes were probably much like those of other whites, especially after the militant Unionists lost their initial influence. As one Mississippi Democrat observed of a rival, "I was a Secessionist for Slavery's sake, and he was a Unionist for the very same. Now, tell me what right he has to your [freedmen's] sympathy and support more than I have." It was a reasonable question. Scalawags' egalitarianism largely consisted of a belief that freedpeople were necessary electoral allies. Otherwise this minority believed they were entitled to political preeminence over a mass following they preferred to hold at arm's length. Tension was inevitable once African Americans realized what sort of allies circumstances had thrust upon them. The underlying problem was that even among white Republicans, racial supremacist views were pervasive. Without the pressure of outright demands, native white Republicans had little to offer blacks beyond the right to vote for them.

The freedpeople initially hesitated to press for black leadership, so they naturally turned to white outsiders of one sort or another. They may not have sought out those most alienated from dominant opinion, but it looked like a healthy sign of racial enlightenment. Militant Unionists benefited from this distrust of the Southern white mainstream, but a preference for newcomers was more apparent. One Louisiana legislator explained his political emergence simply: "The colored people wanted a Northern man for their leader." At the constitutional conventions, recent migrants were elected from plantation districts in far greater numbers than were native whites. More than half of the first cohort of Republican congressmen from the ten reconstructed states had arrived in the South since the start of the war. In Alabama seven of the eight-member initial Republican congressional delegation were recent arrivals, the other one born in Scotland. Such men became prominent in the factional groupings described as "Radical." Northern veterans could reasonably be expected to be anti-slavery by conviction rather than circumstance. They presented themselves as physically and morally braver than their Unionist counterparts, who often had complicated wartime records. The underlying tension is often depicted as a leadership split between rival "scalawag"- and "carpetbag"-led factions, which was indeed a noticeable pattern. Still, ideology or interest-group politics explain more than leadership nativity. Civil rights increasingly drove factional development, and this empowered the black majority and the Radical leaders who spoke for them.

In Virginia these patterns unfolded with revealing speed. African Americans comprised 42 percent of the population, so the Republicans should have been competitive, but dissension brought instant defeat. Opponents didn't even find necessary the scale of terrorist countermobilization evident elsewhere. What happened? Virginia's well-organized black population made a strong bid for influence. Although operating mostly through white intermediaries, the freedpeople insisted that their economic and social agenda shape party policies. But national leaders repeatedly balked at this nearby grassroots insurgency, which deprived Reconstruction of the backing it needed to establish itself.

Virginia's unique situation furthered black politicization. It had the South's major industrial city, with large numbers of pre-war free blacks. Richmond and nearby Petersburg were swollen with freedmen from the war-torn countryside. As was the case in other urban areas after black enfranchisement, dock strikes and occupations of segregated streetcars shook the city, and such labor-tinged activism always raised difficult issues for Republicans. An "ultra" Unionist editor, Reverend James Hunnicutt, orchestrated a popular movement with egalitarian overtones. At an early Republican meeting some speakers talked of land redistribution. Thaddeus Stevens's proposal was not in the national Republican mainstream, at least not this long after the fighting ended, and Radical heavyweights bore these tidings to Virginia. Senator Henry Wilson warned that an all-black party could never rule. Horace Greeley similarly told a Richmond crowd that Congress would never back confiscation.

National leaders sought a different profile. "To organize a campaign on the Hunnicutt plan," Greeley's *Tribune* observed, "is to abandon any hope of a permanent Union party in the South." Northern businessmen arrived to quell dissension, and a subsequent convention was called that highlighted the participation of former Whigs. One favored leader, John Minor Botts, reportedly had stated that he "would let educated monkeys vote if they would help the Republican Party," a wording unlikely to flatter his prospective allies. Not surprisingly, the gathering was tumultuous, and Virginia's early polarization along racial/ideological lines persisted. At the state's protracted constitutional convention, blacks comprised nearly a quarter of the delegates. The ex-slave George Teamoh conceded that white conservatives gave better speeches, but their racial animus was so apparent that his colleagues knew what to do. The result was a proposed constitution that included strong support for education and civil rights. Radicals pressed for disfranchisement of large numbers of ex-Confederate officers as well as limitations on officeholding, and these provisions passed with black support.

The *New York Times* deplored such measures to keep Virginia under the influence of the "Hunnicutt anarchists." Virginia's military commander, General John Schofield, personally urged the delegates to change course, especially on local-control provisions. He predicted that as things stood, illiterate blacks would fill most offices. Fearing the constitution would pass, he concluded "to let the thing fall and die where it is—not submit it to the people at all." He stopped the election on a budgetary pretext, and his superior, general and presidential candidate U. S. Grant, chose not to intervene. Congress could have appropriated funds, but the Republican majority did nothing. Schofield interpreted this as implicit approval, and the constitution stayed in limbo for a year.

By the time Grant took office, the disfranchisement policies pursued by the Virginia convention seemed less timely. Grant asked Congress to authorize a ratification election with the disfranchisement sections voted on separately. Over these provisions, Virginia's Republican party split, mostly along racial lines. Radicals endorsed military governor H. H. Wells while moderates backed another Northerner, Gilbert C. Walker. Under conservative leadership, the opposition tactically endorsed Walker and his "True Republicans," though with evident reluctance. Virginia's conservatives lobbied Grant, declaring their acquiescence to black suffrage, and he was persuaded by the promise of future influence. In the July 1869 elections the excised constitution won approval, and Walker was elected governor along with a predominantly Democratic legislature. Ex-secessionists soon regained supremacy, to preside over the Democrats' own fiscal meltdown, but Radical Reconstruction ended before it began.

Tennessee provided a similar lesson after a beleaguered moderate governor allowed disfranchised ex-Confederates to flood to the polls, a danger endemic to all such policies. The Democratic legislature then called a new constitutional convention and soon solidified control. These reverses colored Grant's position in Republican factional battles that followed. Upon assuming the presidency, Grant encouraged scalawag racial moderates as the sort of propertied, solid leaders he preferred, and the Northern press approved. But without the freedpeople on board there was no Southern party, no possibility of electoral success. Encouraging moderate Republicans pursuing disruptive maneuvers seemed counterproductive, because what tactical white support they won was premised on disrupting the Republican coalition. Thus when Republicans divided, over policy or patronage, the administration increasingly sided with the party's core constituency.

Mississippi demonstrated the new pattern. Congress had the state's defeated Radical constitution resubmitted to the voters late in 1869, with disfranchisement being voted on separately. With Democratic encouragement, conservative Republicans put up an independent ticket, led by, of all people, Grant's brother-in-law. The nepotistic president decided he was being conned, and he endorsed the planter scalawag James Alcorn, who won the governorship by a large margin. Likewise in Texas, Andrew Jackson Hamilton, a wartime Unionist, was running as a moderate Republican with Democratic support. Grant backed the Radical alternative, Edmund J. Davis, who narrowly won the governorship with unified black support. For the president, conciliating white opinion increasingly seemed less of a priority.

President Grant's position was crucial because he controlled the federal bureaucracy, the lifeblood of the formal political process. In this era, control of government employment generally secured the party machinery for whatever ends. Few would lavish much time on party caucuses and rallies without having a personal stake. Because the political culture was rooted in the spoils system, policy debate took place through this ego-drenched medium. Issues were filtered through an intervening step of networked struggles for patronage. The consequences were divisive in the Reconstruction South. Jobs were scarce in the ruined region, and political activists were generally men of modest means. Prominent Republicans, and perhaps whites especially, wanted a personal payoff, some validation for the abuse of themselves and their families. As for the freedmen, government employment became freighted with practical and symbolic civil rights implications.

Factional development often followed a standard pattern. After Reconstruction governments began functioning, moderate Republican governors generally conciliated whites in order to co-opt discontent and pursue economic development. Governors could thereby win some public toleration and press praise, at least personally. As Governor Alcorn observed, leaders charged with "making the principles of a social revolution acceptable to a people of volatile passions" necessarily shrank from unnecessary offense. This "triangulation" strategy demanded distance from black political demands. Whatever the merits of individual issues, the experience never felt good to the victims of political expediency. In particular, bipartisan appointments, on grounds of competency or community acceptability, troubled black activists. Freedmen increasingly sought representation that was accountable to them, African Americans or white allies independent of the statewide power structure.

Federal officeholders frequently stepped into the breach. They were often newcomers, insulated from white opinion. As one Republican recalled, "In the large centers, like New Orleans, the white Republicans were not without pleasant society, but they found it alone in interassociation." To hold their notoriously insecure jobs for themselves and their subordinates, federal officials sought a local constituency, generally the black majority of party supporters. This became the institutional basis of what were termed "Radical/carpetbagger" factions across the South. If Northern-origin Radicals often got the higher positions, African-American preferences determined substantive policies. Black activists tired of being trifled with to suit a tactical agenda, and they looked for someone in authority to speak for them. It may not have been convenient in electoral terms, but freedpeople sought leaders they could trust on their issues.

Factional disputes proliferated, perhaps most spectacularly in Louisiana, though the origins long antedated the Grant administration. Republicans early adopted a policy of parity in representation, mandating that at least half of all party nominees be African American. This assured a direct black voice at the constitutional convention, and Louisiana framed an outright prohibition on racial segregation. Advanced ideas were much in evidence, and the bilingual activists of the *New Orleans Tribune* effectively promoted racial egalitarianism. To run the paper the Afro-Creole owners hired a radical Belgian exile named Jean-Charles Houzeau. He "took delight in openly shaking hands with these outcasts" as a personal protest, and he never contradicted the rumor that he had African ancestry. Houzeau found the misperception "oddly stimulating," a level of empathetic solidarity that was unusual. In particular, it was not to be found in the state's central political figure, Henry Clay Warmoth.

An ambitious Illinois veteran, still in his mid-twenties, Warmoth was nominated governor over one of the *Tribune*'s owners. His memoir derided this opposition, observing that his well-heeled opponents believed "in the Africanization of the State." Warmoth won with support from freedmen, who were somewhat skeptical of elite Afro-Creole leadership, but he antagonized supporters quickly. In his inaugural address he urged lawmakers to trust to time to change the racial climate, and he opposed and vetoed bills enforcing the constitution's open-accommodations provisions. Warmoth instead pursued outreach to

whites and an ambitious economic development program of lev-
ees, railroads, and canals. As the state debt ballooned, African
Americans wondered whose interests were being served.

Federal officeholders provided a well-connected alternative
leadership. Collector of Customs William P. Kellogg was overly
solicitous of black activists, at least according to a disaffected former employee. Kellogg reportedly appointed "a numerous legion
of ignorant, vicious negroes as black as coal," which when trans-
lated might suggest he hired from outside the freeborn elite, an
important point in caste-bound Louisiana. Future senator Kellogg reportedly wined and dined black legislators. He even
allegedly "took them to Public places and in prostitute dens—
matched them with white women, yes, every dirty, foul and vul-
gar trick was played." This self-interested statement may be a
fabrication, but the wider point is that defiance of Southern
racial etiquette and male camaraderie might go a long way in
New Orleans. Legislators could not judge the hearts of their
white allies, could not readily see behind the scenes, but they
could observe how prospective leaders treated them.

Over the next few years, conflict escalated between Governor
Warmoth and a coalescing group of federal officeholders. The
leaders were Senator Kellogg and two other newcomers, U.S.
marshal Stephen Packard and Collector of Customs James F.
Casey, another presidential brother-in-law. The customhouse or
Radical faction distinguished itself with emphatic support for the
Grant administration. Black leaders hesitated at first, but most
gradually moved toward the Radicals. While Warmoth does not
seem to have been generally corrupt, he personally benefited
from any number of government-connected opportunities. People tried to bribe him daily, he admitted. *The Nation* marveled at
such statements, wondering why no one was prosecuted, and
young Warmoth became about the South's most notorious carpetbagger. His style of leadership encouraged the free-spending

legislature, and as national criticism grew, it reinforced the restiveness of black leaders on other grounds.

A bewildering confrontation developed, featuring extensive Washington involvement. Grant was not much impressed with Warmoth, his former subordinate; during the war he had tried to have him dismissed for an indiscreet press interview. The president now reportedly told intimates "that anything was justifiable to overthrow Governor Warmoth." In mid-1871 Collector Casey summoned a Republican convention at the customhouse, and fearing police interference he overawed opponents with Gatling guns. He charged that the governor had appointed to office whites who were not committed to Grant's reelection. Radicals subsequently aligned with Democrats to seek control of the legislature, planning impeachment charges, and rival legislature bodies resulted. At one point Radical legislators were sent offshore to defeat a quorum call, thus improbably involving the navy in Republican factional politics. Collector Casey telegraphed Grant for aid four times in one day, and Marshal Packard arrested Warmoth on civil rights charges. These destabilizing maneuvers were not calculated to inspire respect for either the administration or federal authority. Both sides disgraced the Republican party, the *New York Times* concluded. Northern opinion would be frosty when Grant later intervened in Louisiana with more urgent justification.

Federal employees were calling the tactical shots in this episode, and control of the state's delegation for Grant's renomination probably motivated the contest. But African Americans didn't need persuasion, for they backed the president emphatically. The controversy allowed activists to weigh in under circumstances where black opinion mattered, within the majority party. Also, black leaders on both sides relished being courted. P. B. S. Pinchback, who backed Warmoth, described the African-

American presence at a meeting with the president: "The colered men on the Committee made a fine appearance. . . . They were the observed of all the observers." Pinchback was no idealist, but he professed himself proud of his comrades.

Revealingly, Warmoth emphasized black malevolence rather than his customhouse opposition for his woes. "The spirit of 'San Domingo' showed itself," he wrote. "They criticized my personal associates and alleged that I was trying to get into 'high society.'" Warmoth cited as proof a circular by Lieutenant Governor Oscar Dunn, which charged that the governor privately opposed black officeholding. Warmoth quoted the letter entire in his autobiography, thinking it demonstrated that critics had exploited the race issue. But the statement, by a notably upright black politician, better illustrates the depth of popular disillusionment. Had constituents trusted Warmoth, the customhouse intrigue would hardly have mattered. Disaffection encouraged destabilizing maneuvers, however badly they looked to the external public.

Another cause of factional development has received less notice by modern historians who tend toward an upbeat depiction of Reconstruction. With suffrage, long-standing divisions within the black community became politicized, especially in the cities where factionalism became most intense. The prominence of freeborn leaders raised issues of privilege, and personal rivalries between leaders like the light-skinned moderate Pinchback and the dark-complexioned ex-slave Dunn took on wider connotations. A study of black politicians in New Orleans, for example, found that 90 percent of known background were of mixed ancestry, and 97 percent had been free; twenty of the two hundred had actually owned slaves. The tumult of Republican factionalism invited elements within the black community to challenge their subordinate status. It made for treacherous class terrain. Even Frederick Douglass rejected a career in Southern politics, fearing he sounded too polished: "I could not have readily adapted myself to the peculiar oratory found to be most effective with the newly enfranchised class."

Factional conflict was sometimes so systematic as to force a public airing. Mobile, for example, had many typical urban characteristics. It had a significant freeborn population, some of it Afro-Creole, and a postwar surge of freedpeople settling the outskirts, as Southern cities generally did. Rural in-migration exacerbated class tensions within the black community, many of whose existing residents were settled and relatively prosperous. Military Reconstruction encouraged grassroots activism, including a major dock strike and the occupation of streetcars, culminating in a riot at a Republican rally. Alarmed, the city's few moderate scalawags promoted restrained black leadership who would channel discontent to the political process and the courts. Almost to a man, these preferred moderate spokesmen were freeborn, of mixed ancestry, and quite literate. Their priorities were soon challenged by Radical activists pursuing direct-action tactics. Most of these rival leaders were freedmen, commonly described as black, and they were often recent migrants from the countryside.

Over time, Mobile's division intensified along ideological and social lines. Whites led both factions, but they were thoroughly interracial, for Republican activists were about the most integrated subculture in Southern society. Local controversy linked up with state and national patronage patterns in ways that empowered individual black activists. Alabama's two U.S. senators feuded over Mobile's customhouse, and African Americans had long been irritated by their near exclusion from federal employment. When President Grant appointed ex-senator Willard Warner as collector, Warner hired scores from the moderate group, most prominently the leading Creole politician Philip Joseph. As Warner explained, "The colored people pretty generally asked the appointment of one of their number to some place in the Customs building as a matter of principle." This affirmative-action hiring pleased many, but activists from the Radical faction protested their continued exclusion as elitist. Acrimonious public rallies ensued, a contest that yielded rival candidates and even occasional fisticuffs. A Radical paramilitary, supposedly directed against the Klan, was used against the moderate faction. At one rally everything was quiet as long as the speakers praised Grant, but at Philip Joseph's name a din arose from a nearby Radical band. Years of such Republican infighting occurred in a city in which whites represented a substantial majority.

Factional strife was grounded in the social process of emancipation rather than being conjured by intriguing carpetbaggers. State and national politics shaped the dispute, but the community divisions already existed. Nor was the focus on patronage accidental; activists believed access to federal jobs a legitimate concern. Mobile's activists profited from a bidding war between white politicians, breaching customary patterns of racial and class exclusion. The contest for popular loyalties propelled an escalation of demands. It strengthened grassroots elements most inclined toward labor radicalism and least attuned to outside perception. At least this was the case in Mobile, where moderates generally discouraged direct action but grassroots insurgents had a different profile. The premier Radical leader, Allen Alexander, was a renowned street fighter, arrested repeatedly due to conflicts with other Republicans. The process of popular empowerment may not have been helpful in electoral terms, but it could hardly be avoided. No black leader had so secure a position he could resist the tendency toward more radical demands.

Thus the Southern party moved inexorably toward identification with the popular constituency. Only the Republican leadership in Washington might conceivably have stayed the process or have forced the freedmen to maintain a subordinate posture.

For a while Grant tried, but his experience of moderate defections soured him. Such movements were "intended to carry a portion of the Republican party over to the Democracy, and thus give them controll." Grant's stiffening position may also have reflected his underlying inclination. Upon assuming office he championed the Fifteenth Amendment extending equal suffrage nationwide. Longtime Radical George Boutwell thought the president primarily responsible for its ratification. Frederick Douglass privately contended that Grant "proved himself a better republican than he was supposed to be when first nominated and voted for." Grant was, after all, the hero of the anti-slavery war, and he was prone to elemental loyalties.

Criticism of the administration played into this pattern. Grant quickly disillusioned clean-government enthusiasts and free-traders. In September 1869 the freebooting financiers Jay Gould and Jim Fisk cornered the gold market, with the inside assistance of yet another presidential brother-in-law. Some Republican intellectuals turned their attention to such issues while more advanced reformers joined growing discussion of women's rights. In the *North American Review* the anti-slavery editor Gamaliel Bradford observed that the Fifteenth Amendment concluded the great anti-slavery struggle that had consumed national attention for a generation. Reconstruction was now comparatively "of minor importance." Other problems were pressing for solution, but national leaders were still focused on the South.

Many Northerners agreed with this diagnosis, and the Republicans lost much of their House majority in the fall 1870 elections. Afterward, according to Henry Adams, the possibility of a dissident convention was raised "as a threat over the party." A successful Democrat/Liberal Republican coalition in Missouri furnished the movement a name, a platform, and a national spokesman, Senator Carl Schurz. This became the prototype for a national movement that was the real threat to Grant's presi-

dency, rather than the treason-tainted Democratic party. Opinion leaders flayed corruption, nepotism, and the whole anti-
intellectual style of Washington. The war-bred vogue of activist
government received increasing scrutiny, particularly its tariffs
and railroad subsidies. The leaders were "Liberal" Republicans
in the British sense of laissez-faire, and Grant took their criticism
personally. He reportedly denounced Carl Schurz as an atheist.
Grant admitted to "a repugnance to the appointment of an
Adams which I would not feel to . . . an out-and-out Democrat."
After Senator Sumner frustrated a pet project to annex Santo
Domingo, Grant rebuffed mediation, calling the longtime Radical "unreasonable, cowardly, slanderous, unblushingly false."

Liberal Republican criticism interacted in a complex, recip-
rocal fashion with the woes of the opposition Democrats. After
losing several elections on the Southern/race issue, previously intransigent Democratic leaders, led by the reviled copperhead
Clement Vallandigham, called for accepting the constitutional
amendments. This was indeed a New Departure, given previous
Democratic racial extremism. Southern spokesmen resisted the
trend, but most capitulated to Northern pressure. New York's
spectacular Tweed Ring scandals of 1871 reinforced Democratic
pliancy, but Horatio Seymour saw a silver lining in his party's
public humiliation: "When the public mind is turned to the
question of frauds, etc., etc., there will be a call for the books at
Washington as well as in the city of New York."

Talk of corruption and other liberal issues influenced Southern policy in complex ways. Liberal critics of Grant did not initially target the freedpeople. Free trade, amnesty, and civil
service reform were their main concerns. Many had been Radical Republicans, like Senator Schurz himself. Godkin's *Nation*,
for example, endorsed federal open-accommodations laws.
Grant nonetheless perceived an analogy between his Republican
critics and Southern factional woes. The third-party scenario

had become thoroughly familiar, especially since the Liberal Republican platform and its leading spokesman hailed from a border state. Defectors would soon see that the Missouri bolt led "just where the Tenn. and Va. bolts did," in ex-Rebel takeovers. National developments reinforced Grant's enthusiasm for the regular Republicans in the South.

As the Liberal revolt developed, black leaders were placed in a difficult situation. Frederick Douglass had spent his adult life in reform circles, and now his trusted comrades like Charles Sumner opposed Grant. As America's leading black intellectual, Douglass's personal role was crucial, and he responded decisively. He tethered Republicans anew to African-American concerns through emphatic partisan loyalty. His paper editorially opposed civil service reform along with "every other device to demoralize and break up the grandest political organization that ever existed in this country." He also saw the cause of civil rights as vitally tied to Northern memories of the war: "Talk of dead issues! The Republican party will have living issues with the Democratic party until the last rebel is dead and buried." Douglass denounced the notion of universal amnesty as a humanitarian chimera. He even accompanied the presidential commission to Santo Domingo, and he endorsed Grant's unpopular purchase proposal. Douglass anticipated black opinion in full-throated endorsement of Grant's leadership.

The Ku Klux Klan issue encouraged this response. By this point the fun-and-games interpretation of the Klan had worn thin. State courts were clearly incapable of bringing the perpetrators to justice, for almost never did Southern juries convict any Klansmen. State governments had limited options. In some places governors mobilized state militias, with mixed results. In Arkansas, Governor Powell Clayton shut down the Klan quickly after one substantial confrontation. Tennessee's predominantly Unionist militia restored order but absorbed a substantial share

of the state's budget. But arming and deploying state forces antagonized most whites. In North Carolina, Governor Holden
called out the interracial militia, but arrests of dubious legality
lost his party the legislative elections of 1870 and got him impeached. South Carolina's Governor Scott ordered out the overwhelmingly black militia before his reelection that same year, but
this inflamed white fears, which encouraged Klan activities
where the upland demographics permitted it. For this reason
moderate Republican governors like Alcorn in Mississippi and
Smith in Alabama refused to arm freedmen. Moderate leaders
also opposed federal legislation, hoping that local elites might
handle the problem, but wealthy scalawags seldom felt the
Klan's full fury. Desperate Republicans in the countryside demanded protection.

With presidential encouragement, Congress passed enforcement acts giving federal courts power to try crimes against voters, a substantial expansion in government responsibility. In early
1871 Grant came into one cabinet meeting bearing depressing reports. He suggested transferring troops from the Texas frontier,
observing it made no sense to protect white Southerners who
were making more trouble than the Indians. The cabinet discussed sending black regiments into South Carolina. Two members thought it would "encourage the Negro population, and
give them more courage and self-reliance." Others feared it
would inflame the whites, and if it miscarried, would backfire
with the Northern public. Grant concluded to send other troops,
but it is striking that his advisers discussed encouraging the
freedpeople to fight back.

They might have rethought that notion a few weeks later, after a bloody riot in Meridian, Mississippi. Klansmen raided from
Sumter County across the Alabama border after absconding laborers, and freedmen mobilized to resist. When black officeholders were assassinated outside town, an angry leader made a

public threat to burn Meridian, and someone set a fire that night. The nominally Republican mayor ordered the arrest of black leaders, and a trainload of Klansmen arrived for the trial. A courtroom scuffle occurred, and it appears one defendant, while under assault, fired a shot that killed the judge. Armed Klansmen opened up from the back of the courtroom, and they lynched people for hours, now as a nominal posse. Save for the judge, every fatality was black, ten or more, three as captives. Rioters seized a train and pursued a fleeing black legislator, and they burned his house and a church. Klansmen then returned home, shooting a black girl from the train for sport, according to a Democratic paper.

It was the sort of atrocity to concentrate the public mind, prompting reconsideration of traditional notions of local control. Grant urged legislation, which passed quickly. The Ku Klux or Enforcement act expanded federal authority to prosecute violation of voters' civil rights, trying them before a loyal jury. It gave the president temporary powers to detain suspects without charge. A region-wide manhunt followed enactment. In Alabama alone, several hundred Klansmen were indicted. That fall the administration made an example of western South Carolina, suspending habeas corpus in nine counties. Attorney General Amos Akerman oversaw hundreds of detentions to prevent escapes or the murder of witnesses. Southern white opinion combined high-voltage outrage at Grant's tyranny with a practical awareness that it was time to stand down. Numbers fled, and the Klan ceased to function almost everywhere in time for the 1872 election. Black leaders were gleeful; it was as if someone had pulled a plug on terrorism.

These measures were unprecedented in peacetime. For Liberal Republicans the Klan issue posed difficult problems. Reform leaders backed the Fifteenth Amendment, hoping to guarantee black rights without endlessly propping up flawed

Republican regimes. But the constitutional concerns raised by the Klan legislation troubled them, and general amnesty was the liberals' preferred solution, the one that would hopefully solve the underlying problem of Southern misrule. *The Nation* wrote, "it is perhaps better that the outrages should continue till the necessity of ending them unites the decent and respectable citizens of each State." Such restraint little commended itself to Klan victims, but for the reformers that was secondary. Schurz wrote E. L. Godkin, "I was glad to see the *Nation* strike so vigorously at the insane Ku-Klux legislation now under discussion in Congress." With the Democrats publicly endorsing the New Departure, the Klan issue provided common ground for all administration opponents.

The issue was even more welcome for the administration. It rallied freedmen to Grant; it roused them to risk the polls as nothing else could. The immediate results made the anti-Klan laws even more appealing. Mississippi's Senator Adelbert Ames wrote that the prosecutions had a subduing effect across the South. Ames even began speaking before white crowds, and "Had it not been for the Ku Klux law which we fought for and which the Governor [Alcorn] fought against, we would not have had any showing at this election." Blacks universally favored the anti-Klan laws, and being in complete accord on the defining issue of Grant's reelection encouraged unity on lesser matters. When the principled Senator Sumner started pushing open-accommodations legislation, he found his black colleagues quietly unsupportive. For the time being, Grant's vague assurances sufficed.

The Ku Klux issue concentrated Northern attention on favorable ground. By all accounts the debates and hearings over the measure finally galvanized opinion. Rutherford B. Hayes proclaimed it the foremost national issue; everything else was subordinate for Northerners who had opposed slavery and backed the Union cause. Federal intervention simultaneously counteracted the Democratic predominance in the Southern press. Federal troops and trials provided outside verification of the violence, and a congressional investigating committee took eleven volumes of eyewitness testimony. The news featured a daily diet of horrors, and even Grant's Northern critics conceded the reality. As *The Nation* resignedly observed, as long as violence was met with "mealy-mouthed censure from Southern conservatives," Northern moderates couldn't provide much help.

The Klan issue, combined with the Tweed Ring scandals, yielded sweeping Democratic defeats in the fall of 1871. Grant became confident of reelection, but his critics thought differently. In Schurz's enthusiastic estimate, Democratic collapse would force a coalition on dissidents' terms. When Grant's renomination became obvious, the liberals already had one foot out the door. In the spring of 1872 thousands gathered in Cincinnati to found the Liberal Republican party. They endorsed a platform of universal suffrage and amnesty, and called on those of all political backgrounds to join them. The journalistic sponsors of the movement lost control of the mass convention, and an embarrassingly obvious deal nominated Horace Greeley in exchange for a vice-presidential nomination for another contender, Governor B. Gratz Brown of Missouri. Liberal leaders had been courting the influential editor, but now to their bewilderment Greeley emerged as the nominee.

Greeley had baggage. He had been an abolitionist and then a Radical Republican, both of which credentialed him with Republicans. But the editor also had espoused every reform from vegetarianism to utopian socialism. He was perhaps the nation's leading protectionist spokesman, in a movement mostly devoted to free trade. As Charles Francis Adams, Jr., bitterly observed, "we came back with the great apostle of unlimited legislation on all conceivable subjects for our chosen candidate." Greeley had even endorsed the Ku Klux Klan act before breaking with Grant. Then there was the matter of Greeley's personal appearance: his trademark white hat and coat made for cartoonist ridicule. In long tirades Schurz urged the candidate to withdraw, and E. L. Godkin wailed, "Is there no way out of the wretched mess into which these Cincinnati nominations have plunged us?" His *Nation* disgustedly endorsed the reelection of President Grant.

The Democrats were more composed. Nominating Horace Greeley on a platform of universal amnesty and suffrage might eliminate the wartime issues once and for all. Besides, Greeley ran on the evils of carpetbag rule and federal bayonets, and Southern leaders appreciated his call to "clasp hands across the bloody chasm." The idealistic editor had once helped bail Jefferson Davis from jail, a position that entailed considerable Northern abuse and financial loss. It thus meant something when he preached reconciliation: "They talk about Rebels and traitors. Fellow-citizens, are we never to be done with this?" At the Democratic convention some holdouts hoped that another choice might be insisted upon, and Greeley himself admitted that the reluctant endorsement did not gratify his ego. But the weakened Democrats would do anything to beat Grant.

Greeley supporters expected inroads into the black vote. Charles Sumner and other prominent abolitionist leaders supported Greeley, and early Liberal Republican meetings had second-tier African-American leaders in attendance. But once Democratic support became evident, black interest melted away. Small wonder, with publications like the *Lexington Caucasian* endorsing Greeley, for it didn't take many indiscreet Democrats to undermine his appeal. As one puzzled barber remarked, "I can't see how a Republican can be running on a Democratic ticket. There is something loose somewhere." Few slaves had read the *New York Tribune*, but freedmen knew all about General Grant.

Greeley encountered outright hostility, reportedly including a death threat from one woman. His bitter conclusion was that blacks "as a class, are steeled against us. They will not hear us."

It was a fateful choice for African Americans. The alliance with the administration placed them in company with unsavory partisans of the spoils system. With the advantage of hindsight, one can wonder if freedpeople would have done well to respond differently. If their rights were assured, Sumner now thought, blacks should not "band together in a hostile camp, provoking antagonism and keeping alive the separation of races." Given how soon Reconstruction unraveled, this might have been an opportunity to reach out to the eventual ruling class. One can imagine alternative scenarios flowing from a Greeley victory. The New Departure had Southern advocates, and encouraging them might have been judicious, opportunistic though they might be. But few freedmen hesitated to back a popular president who had just shut down the Klan. One black politician dismissed Greeley's anti-slavery record: "No, the mass of [freedmen] don't know anything about it; and if they did, they would not support a man, no matter who, that the Democrats support." Thus Frederick Douglass spoke for a united following: "I had better put a gun to my head and blow my brains out, than to lend myself in any wise to the destruction or defeat of the republican party."

Concerned over possible black defections, and for once immune to Democratic race baiting, the Republicans embraced civil rights. One campaign document, *The Struggle for '72*, illustrates the themes. The work reported on the number of blacks who held federal jobs, finding 250 in one Washington bureau alone. It also noted black oratory as a "peculiar feature" of the Republican national convention, and as for the platform, "the most important question was that of reconstruction, and upon this the Southern delegates were clamorous for something radical and unequivocal." The Republican platform was otherwise startlingly opportune. It denounced the spoils system and endorsed civil service reform; it also endorsed the principle of universal amnesty. Congress, at Grant's urging, had just lifted the Fourteenth Amendment's officeholding restrictions on nearly all ex-Confederate leaders. This eliminated one of the Liberals' popular issues, for only in Arkansas were numbers of ex-Confederates still disfranchised. As one observer commented, the platform "leaves the Cincinnati crowd nothing to fight for—nothing but Greeley and Gratz."

Political observers predicted a close election, or even that Greeley would win. Seldom have pundits misread opinion so completely, especially with respect to civil service reform, which appealed primarily to elites. Northern Democrats had trouble swallowing their longtime tormentor, Greeley. As Horatio Seymour privately groused, "I can see my way clear to vote for him, as he can be made of use in driving negroes out of office, but it is hard to speak for him." Seymour's tone suggests the other problem: the manifest opportunism of the New Departure. Greeley's initial support was premised on the Democrats somehow fading away. That was never their intent, and the subsequent Democratic endorsement compromised his initial appeal. "Our [Republican] party ought, perhaps, not to succeed now," the reform-minded James Garfield wrote, "but the combination against us was so absurd and so wicked as to make our party relatively high toned and noble." Seldom has a candidate reaped such anti-intellectual ridicule as the articulate editor. By late summer, state elections suggested a sweeping Republican triumph. Even the initial revelations of the Credit Mobilier scandal made little impression, and a resurgence of open terrorism that summer in Georgia only roused Northern resentment. Grant rolled up 55.6 percent of the popular vote, the largest portion for decades in a postwar era of close elections. The electoral count was a true drubbing; Greeley lost every Northern state.

The newly elected House would be Republican by better than two to one, with the Senate margin nearly as great. Greeley, crushed by the results, died soon after the election.

The Southern results were revealing in the closest thing to a fair election under the Fifteenth Amendment for nearly a century to come. Greeley made no inroads into the black vote, and among whites he ran far behind the typical Democratic vote. The lapse of Klan terror emboldened Unionists, and as the national landslide became clear, many white Democrats stayed home. Conciliatory New Departure rhetoric did not rouse the Democratic masses. As one Southern newspaper had predicted, "It is all we can do to carry our elections here with the magic rallying-cry of a white man's government," and without that talisman Democrats could not win. Greeley carried just Tennessee, Georgia, and Texas among the eleven ex-Confederate states. Republicans even made something of a comeback at the state level, regaining governorships in Alabama and North Carolina and congressional seats elsewhere.

It appeared that Republican defeats weren't irreversible if the federal government enforced equal suffrage. Something like normal two-party competition appeared possible as a continuing reality. Dispirited Democrats threw up their hands, and reasonable people thought the Reconstruction settlement would persist indefinitely. As the *New York Times* concluded, "Whatever party may rule, equality, civil and political, before the law, can never be overthrown without another war." Because African-American leaders had negotiated factional politics so effectively, Reconstruction had a few more years to become established. Even in the already Democratic states, the threat of renewed national intervention discouraged provocative behavior. For several years, social development proceeded on this transformed basis, as whites and blacks tried to negotiate their daily reality on these unaccustomed terms.

7

Gender, Race, and Civil Society in the Reconstruction South

DESCRIBING CIVIL SOCIETY during Republican Reconstruction is complex because of the shifting picture of violence and benign daily life. Terror was an overriding social reality across large rural areas. It was pervasive in some localities, episodic in others, and for victims it was the overriding concern. The natural tendency has been for historians to focus upon these dramatic aspects. Still, the violence ebbed and flowed, and for much of the time it receded in people's consciousness. By the early 1870s relative stability and economic recovery characterized much of the South, and national political currents worked to the freedpeople's advantage. An uneven normalization of daily life took place on the basis of free labor and black political influence. Thus in those places where the Reconstruction regime was stable, freedpeople could capitalize on the dramatic change in their civil status. Reconstruction afforded them unprecedented influence over the structure of law and public life. It proved temporary, but it mattered, and it had social consequences even after Reconstruction was overthrown.

Gender is one area in which postwar changes in civil society proceeded apace. Lack of suffrage somewhat insulated freedwomen from formal politics, but changes affecting women, work, and the family were political in the broad sense. Republican law-makers sought to regularize the family status of freedpeople and to reverse the informal practices of slavery, which after all had given slave families no legal recognition. Formal mechanisms were suddenly brought to bear on matters like marriage and divorce. Given the customary practices of the slave quarters, and the prevailing distrust of formal law in such personal matters, this transition was not simple. The recent literature suggests a selective adaptation to Victorian norms. Persistent racial stereotypes on such charged issues did nothing to ease the process. As Ella Clanton Thomas observed with ugly candor, "The majority of us expect no more virtue from our Negro men and women than we do from our horses and cows." Such beliefs pushed ex-slaves toward the recognized norms of freedom.

For all the favorable changes emancipation brought to freedwomen's lives, there was little to empower them relative to freedmen. The old regime, after all, had imposed on slave women a certain harsh gender equality, with the enforced assurance of work, food, and housing if a relationship went bad. Emancipation and suffrage bolstered the position of black men as heads of the family, and the retreat of freedwomen from the fields had a similar effect. But not all relationships were stable, and women without partners had limited options. Fertility had always provided much of slave women's value, and now women with children found few employment opportunities. As one North Carolina planter observed of his male-depleted workforce, "I cannot afford to keep them, and am loath to drive them away. The County Courts will I think find it necessary to bind out the children in very numerous instances and then the women may manage to shift [for] themselves." For many freedwomen with responsibilities, emancipation posed practical issues of survival.

These postwar trends complicate modern expectations of progress over time toward gender equality, and they worked in a somewhat analogous fashion with elite white women. The circumstances were wholly different: elite women tried to preserve a highly gendered life of ease. Whatever frustrations slaveholding women had experienced, especially over issues of sexual privilege, slavery had made possible their well-appointed lives. Women's rights ideas, moreover, were associated with Northern abolitionists like Elizabeth Cady Stanton and Susan B. Anthony. Still, the Civil War scrambled accustomed gender roles. The departure of able-bodied men forced wealthy women into oversight of the slaves, and most found this version of tumult-filled liberation unwelcome. At war's end the inclination was to withdraw into the comforts of their traditional role.

Circumstances thus pushed both freedwomen and their former mistresses toward the ideal of separate spheres. But emancipation transformed their relationship to each other, and household labor illuminates these evolving roles in a practical context. Before the war the use of slave domestics in elite households had been universal. This placed mistresses in closer day-to-day relations with slaves than their husbands generally experienced. Mary Chesnut's famous wartime diary, for example, finds her gossiping with her domestics, acting as occasional marital adviser, and even relying on their support as the Yankees approached. Chesnut regarded her domestics as convenient emotional satellites, lively subordinates who she, happily, could order about.

From the domestics' point of view, things were not so friendly; their lives distilled slavery's infuriating mixture of intimacy and oppression. The disproportionate number of free blacks of mixed racial ancestry itself suggests one dimension. There is a world of evidence of sexual contact involving slave domestics, on terms that suggest coercive abuse. Mary Chesnut herself emphasized the prevalence of interracial liaisons, but she saw the problem as somehow the domestics' fault. Virtuous slaveholding women lived "surrounded by prostitutes" who tempted

their weak men. The slaves perceived the responsibility differently. As Harriet Jacobs's candid autobiography dramatizes, the
Big House was a scene of frequent sexual harassment, and slave
accounts bristle with vengeful mistresses. One ex-slave recalled
that when cooks had mixed-race children, sometimes "the wife
would be mean to them." If the offspring "had nice hair she
would cut it off and wouldn't let them wear it long like white
children." Sexual rivalry combined with forced housework from
reluctant laborers yielded capricious violence. One Virginia
freedwoman recalled an ill-conceived experiment with makeshift
eye makeup; her mistress interpreted it as mockery and decked
her cold. Of those domestics who were old enough to have experienced slavery in all its rigor, many recalled violence at the hands
of mistresses.

When freedom came, domestics responded with everything
from compassion to a feeling of just deserts. One Alabama mistress recalled that when a favored domestic fled, she took only
her mistress's prized possessions, which suggests the motivation
was payback as much as appropriation. For months thereafter
the seething mistress saw her former clothing all over Huntsville,
and one freedwoman helpfully enlightened her on the fate of her
undergarments. "You may imagine what a desecration it seemed,
that that great black Negro should be wearing my handsome
wedding clothes." Emancipation played out differently along
gender lines because elite women were expected to oversee
household tasks. Some found their new duties impossible, like
the newly destitute widow Cornelia Peake McDonald. She pondered having to dismiss her servant amid forebodings of death,
and the two topics seemed connected in her despair. When she
tried to cook, she nearly set her clothes on fire, and she disabled
herself for weeks with a pot of boiling water.

One Baptist prayed: "Give us proper servants, and deliver us
from the evil, the unfaithful, the destructive, and the slothful."

Maria Taylor's resort to the celestial employment agency was unique, but her urgency wasn't. Contemporaries frequently asserted that ex-slaveholding women experienced a tougher transition than their men. One woman knew how to cook fancy recipes, but she had no idea how to boil vegetables. Many could not afford any domestic help, nor could they count on those they did hire. Emma Holmes wrote of legions of fragile women cooking and washing without a murmur. Another Charleston woman told of an acquaintance nearly out of clothes who had, when ill, to "borrow necessities from Sister as sometimes the Negroes won't wash her things for her." One might speculate as to what items, but the woman indignantly concluded, "Is it not a perfect shame?"

These complaints were nearly universal. In South Carolina, Esther Palmer's experience is illustrative. One couple agreed to work for her as domestics, but they quickly concluded they could do better in the fields. Peggy had already left, Lucy was restive over absent children, and Tenny wanted a shortened work week, a request that struck the mistress as presumptuous. Other domestics left to pursue apparent romances, and still others were acting like they intended to leave. This litany occurred in just one letter, and while the immediacy lessened over time, the issue remained pressing. In mid-1870 Samuel Strudwick wrote that the central Alabama plantation belt had been wrecked, but he spent more time complaining about the servants. Wages were cheap enough, but domestics left *without notice*, just when the notion takes them, and leave the burthen to fall on the mistress."

Some former owners hung on to their servants tenaciously. One Mississippi ex-slave recalled, "I stayed with my white folks three years after freedom, and they tried to make me think I wasn't free." Domestics often hesitated to assert their liberty, for connections with powerful whites might prove useful in a disorderly time. One ex-slave recalled that because she lived in the

master's house, other blacks were reluctant to say anything before her. This social isolation complicated departure, so real freedom came after considerable jostling. Multitudes took flight
without explanation since avoiding open confrontation was wisdom as practiced in the slave quarters. One mistress complained
that a favored domestic, who had nursed her lovingly in her recent illness, quit in response to her husband's pressure. The conflicted servant departed without a word.

But freedwomen kept coming back, if not to the same household then to others. Whites could generally hire servants, but
freedwomen's family responsibilities made for skittish workers.
This state of affairs strengthened their bargaining power, and
employers frequently described servants walking off in a huff.
Emancipation brought poor women into elite homes on terms
that smacked of relative equality, or at least of earnest negotiation on the basis of free labor. As the Mississippi Radical A. T.
Morgan observed, mistresses couldn't use "good old time" force-
ful methods with domestics, simply because Grant was president. Klan-style intimidation seldom reached into the Big
House. And because married women gravitated toward family-
based tenant farming, domestics tended to be single or in less stable circumstances. A conflict of values and interests resulted,
often involving issues of family adjustment being worked out in
the legal sphere.

Ex-mistresses were expansive on their discomfort. Ella Clanton Thomas's servants peopled her opiate-laced dreams. She accepted emancipation, but the personal lives of her employees
troubled her. She told her husband that they ought not to allow
one couple to live together, but he forbade interference fearing
disruption of his labor force. Their teenage son then piped in,
"Why Ma . . . None of them are married who are living in the
yard"—a precocious observation that could not have pleased her.
Ella Thomas found herself sorting through such tangled issues a

lot. She once persuaded a cohabiting servant that she ought to divorce her previous husband and remarry, until legal consultation revealed the prohibitive cost. Thomas claimed little taste for such involvement, but on another occasion she transcribed the romantic correspondence of a recently hired servant, Martha. The employer negotiated a wedding date with the groom, wrote out invitations, and provided the wedding site. She even toasted the bride with a "most detestable drink of claret." Thomas described such activities as necessary to keep her domestics comfortably working in her home.

Reluctantly, Ella Thomas was sorting out the gender relations appropriate to emancipation. She engaged in dialogue across racial lines about how family life might now proceed. The disapproving Baptist Maria Taylor similarly gave Affy and Grant "a talk about their intended marriage, and my conditions of receiving her in the yard again," topping it off with a gift of wedding clothes to the groom. In areas peripheral to the work process, one can see such negotiation between women as a daily reality. Other aspects of the employer-employee relationship were more directly adversarial. In agriculture, tenant farming somewhat insulated freedwomen from white employers, but in domestic labor, tension remained endemic. Impoverished former masters could not readily pay wages high enough to provide much motivation, resulting in a continual exodus of dissatisfied servants.

Political consciousness sharpened the confrontation, for slaveholding women were widely regarded as emphatic Confederate holdouts. One memorably proclaimed, "All honor to J[ohn]. Wilkes Booth," a sentiment that was not unusual. Household service often looked like a domestic continuation of the war's issues. Mary Chesnut told a story of a fleeing slave who had difficulty persuading her son to leave their mistress. The mother was "whipping this screaming little rebel darky every foot of the way." The conflation of personal and Confederate loyalty here is clear, and domestics often bore the immediate brunt of white political frustration. Elite women talked a lot about race war. One wealthy South Carolinian believed the right to vote could never be taken from freedmen except through a sea of blood. She concluded, without visible discomfort, that that prospect was approaching. Just before the 1868 election, Ella Thomas and her employees were talking over a threatened riot in nearby Augusta. Perhaps in response to her husband's belligerency, the freedpeople speculated on how well she would acquit herself in battle. Thomas was verbally game rather than intimidated, at least in her account. Still, as she put it, "the idea flashed across my mind of my being a suppliant for mercy at their hands. . . ."

Employers felt powerless. One Savannah physician wrote of his cook, Betty, who was stricken with cholera. She, fortunately in his view, was an "independent Nigger living in her own house," but the tone indicates resentment of her living arrangements. Continuing tension illustrates how much the terms of engagement had changed, and white women gradually learned to do without as much freedwomen's labor. Jane Turner Censer's recent study of elite women discerns a generational shift as labor-saving devices gradually came into use. The younger generation prided themselves on their liberation from old-style dependence upon servants. One might suppose that younger women adapted to new tasks and were physically less dependent on outside help. At the same time live-in domestics became scarce as African-American women set priorities on their own needs. Servants remained common, but the work configuration became less reminiscent of slavery. An intimate Reconstruction occurred under the very noses of the elite.

Like the contemporary shift toward sharecropping on the plantations, domestic labor illustrates a pervasive pattern. Under the umbrella of legal equality, the ex-slaves could reshape their lives, impoverished though they might be. In areas most amenable to formal law, it made a real difference, especially where Reconstruction was relatively stable by virtue of large black majorities. One can trace a democratizing influence across a wide swath of public life. Tax-supported education provides the most obvious example. Within a few years the schools were producing multitudes of young freedpeople with basic skills. The impact mounted over time as the community gained access to literacy. The process can only have bolstered their capacity to function independently.

While it is not true that Reconstruction commenced Southern public education, Republican rule made free schools a systematic policy rather than an indulgence to paupers. After the war, illiteracy among adult white males hovered in the high teens in most states while in North Carolina, according to the 1870 census, a striking 23.7 percent could not write. The war trashed Southern school systems, and hard-pressed Presidential Reconstruction governments were not likely to expand educational opportunities, even for whites. As for African Americans, in 1860 Georgia had reported seven free blacks in public school, Florida nine, and Mississippi two, an effective measure of underlying community support. While there was some talk of schools among Whiggish planters, most whites rejected the notion as dangerous, and virtually nothing was done. Freedpeople actually paid poll taxes earmarked for whites-only schools. Worse, Northern freedmen's aid societies confronted widespread hostility in the South. One Alabama schoolteacher received a threat so mind-bogglingly obscene that the substance cannot be conveyed in print, even now. An important start was made, but five years after the war more than 90 percent of adult black males in the ex-Confederate states still could not write.

The priority was to create permanent, tax-supported public school systems with the promise of universal access. Northern benevolent contributions were drying up, and most Freedmen's

Bureau functions ceased at the end of 1868, so the urgency seemed apparent. Although building and staffing schools took time, and funding shortfalls undermined ambitious plans, Republicans pursued the initiative avidly. Governor Powell Clayton of Arkansas recalled it was the issue he personally cared most about. Some critics have emphasized that the teaching was laden with Yankee notions of hard work, temperance, and other themes appropriate for working-class edification and Victorian gender roles. Still, whatever the formal curriculum, the insight that basic skills empowered people must be right.

In building schools and sustaining teachers, lawmakers created one of Reconstruction's lasting positive legacies. Public education disseminated basic literacy through much of the younger generation. For all its financial woes, South Carolina saw its student population quadruple under Republican rule. Nothing like full access was achieved, but by the mid-1870s, in several states, half the school-age children of both races attended primary schools. By 1880 literacy among adult black males had generally doubled from a decade earlier, with percentages moving into the high twenties among the younger generation. Literacy among black girls became more common than for boys, a reversal of the previous pattern with important social implications. The widely dispersed character of the rural population and school construction costs made even these achievements expensive. Even so, Democratic claims of extravagant funding are probably wrong. In several states these results were achieved at a fraction of the per-student prewar cost, that is, in comparison to the elite-directed schools that had existed with some state aid. In Louisiana, postwar funding *per student* declined by more than two-thirds in constant dollars. Seldom does government undertake so successful an intervention; popular education was achieved at bargain prices.

The education campaign had other ambitious goals. America's historically black colleges were mostly founded during this period, with a combination of public funding and Northern philanthropic aid. Howard University, Fisk University, and Atlanta University all provided accessions to the talented tenth, with long-term implications. Republicans also opened some white colleges to blacks, most prominently the University of South Carolina but also the University of Arkansas. These controversial initiatives had mixed results. In New Orleans, for example, African-American leaders pressed to enforce the constitutional ban on segregated education. After lawsuits, boycotts, and resistance, the courts upheld the provision, and about a third of the city's schools were desegregated for several years. The superintendent received numerous threats, but he was surprised at how well desegregation worked out, and some native whites like the writer George Washington Cable agreed. Such initiatives arguably pushed the envelope in a positive direction, showing whites that there were worse possibilities than segregated free schools. Also, the implementation of black education effectively forced provisions for poorer white children. Thus in 1872 the Mississippi superintendent noted a "most marvelous revolution in public sentiment" during the past year. Here, at least, the Reconstruction shock therapy worked as proponents hoped. Democrats regaining power sometimes shut down school systems on fiscal grounds, for one year in Alabama and for two in Arkansas, but national outrage and local sentiment soon forced resumption. This policy innovation proved irreversible.

Mass education required money, and fiscal policy demonstrated the revolutionary transformation that came with universal suffrage. The black congressman John Roy Lynch observed that building Mississippi schools "required a very large outlay of cash in the beginning, which resulted in a material increase in the rate of taxation. . . ." Schools required a consistent revenue stream, in a region that had long functioned with minimal taxation. Of course there were other mounting costs in state government, but the schools represented a major item of ongoing expense. Overall, taxation more than doubled between 1860 and 1870 in the ex-Confederate states. There would also be a large increase in bonded debt and contingent railroad liability. Republican governments raised most of their revenue through taxation of land as opposed to corporate enterprise or other alternatives. As South Carolina Governor Franklin Moses observed, "The taxes fall chiefly where they belong—upon real estate." This would compel the sale of idle lands, he thought, so that the masses would become property holders. Although the effectiveness as land reform is not clear, the shift in tax policy was pronounced.

Property tax rates escalated sharply. Just to provide the existing level of services, taxes would have had to go up after the war, given the increased number of free citizens, the elimination of taxes on slave property, and the decline in land values. There were burned courthouses and bridges and other necessary infrastructure repairs, along with inflation. Even so, the changes under Republican Reconstruction were pronounced. According to J. Mills Thornton's calculations, Louisiana's property tax per hundred dollars of assessed wealth rose from 29 cents in the late 1850s to $1.45 in 1874, a fivefold increase. Almost everywhere, land taxes grew during Reconstruction by a factor of four or more over prewar levels. Local and municipal levies, often at comparable levels, increased similarly. Even after these increases, state tax rates remained moderate by national standards, but the change in policy was hard to miss.

Mississippi's case is revealing. Here the tax rate swelled from 16 cents per hundred dollars in 1857 to $1.25 in 1873, a nearly eightfold increase. After the depression of the mid-1870s hit, much of the underutilized land in the state would be seized for taxes—by official estimates one-fifth of the state's acreage. None of this commended Reconstruction to Mississippi's property holders. But according to most contemporaries and nearly all historians, the conduct of Mississippi's state government was relatively honest. There were few expensive state-level scandals and few railroad subsidies. Mississippi came out of Republican rule with nominal debt, having chosen a pay-as-you-go policy. With little corruption, the state tax rate presumably represented what it actually cost to fund Reconstruction's expanded programs.

To a striking extent, tax policy reflected the needs of African-American constituents, more than those even of other Republicans. Most white Republicans owned small farms, and given their modest cash incomes they felt property taxes severely. Nonetheless Republican governments never crafted revenue policies that exempted small landownings, seldom even considered them. South Carolina's constitution, for example, provided that subject property be taxed according to its value, which would presumably bar progressive levies. These policies are striking, given Republicans' eager courtship of poorer white voters on economic justice grounds. It highlights how identified the party was with the needs of its core landless constituency on this fundamental issue. Overall, Reconstruction weakened the influence of landowners, which furthered spending priorities toward egalitarian objectives. The consequences are apparent across the region, but they were most obviously transformative in South Carolina.

In Congressman Robert Elliott's somewhat indiscreet estimate, the state had "a Constitution made for the negro by the negro." South Carolina suffered endemic problems of malfeasance but simultaneously had an energized black majority who could shape public policy. Neither aspect much pleased the Democrats, or the Northern public for that matter, but for modern observers a nuanced evaluation is necessary. Social policies sound rather enlightened, at least in aspiration. According to the state constitution, local governments were to provide for "all those inhabitants who, by virtue of age and infirmities or misfortunes" had a claim on society's sympathy. In the mid-1870s

Charleston reportedly provided sixteen hundred poor with out-
door relief. For all its financial woes, South Carolina actually established its insane asylum, institutions for the blind and deaf,
and a state prison during this period. Given the vast number of
sick and elderly ex-slaves, the humanitarian rationale for expanded social spending seems plausible.

The state's unique experiment in land reform illustrates how
Reconstruction changed public goals. It is certainly true, as many
modern historians have observed, that Radical Reconstruction
left the land tenure system intact. If forty acres and a mule were
the prerequisites of genuine liberation, the Republicans never secured them to freedmen, never really made the attempt. In most
states Republicans trusted to tax policy to make plantation land
available, or to federal homestead legislation, with limited practical results. But the situation in South Carolina was different because of the state's lopsided demographics and the wartime
experience of the Union-occupied sea islands. General Sherman's
confiscation orders had an impact long after pardoned planters
got their land back under Andrew Johnson. Once Congressional
Reconstruction began, the freedpeople hoped that the promised
farms would finally materialize.

The South Carolina Land Commission resulted, a unique innovation in Southern governance. The agency's mandate was to
purchase plantations with state funds, divide them into small
farms, and sell them on installment to small farmers. Unfortunately the state's poor credit made the program expensive, and
the commissioners overseeing the process included problematic
officials like Governor Scott and future governor Moses. Planters
routinely gave bribes for inflated appraisals, adding to the purchase costs. Despite this sorry record, after exposure the agency
had success under the upright Francis Cardozo and his successor.
One modern study concludes that over Reconstruction some
14,000 families received farms totaling over 112,000 acres. This

would have represented about 70,000 people, on the order of one-sixth of the black population. Not all these families paid off their loan, but a sample of those occupying land by 1872 indicates that most were still there eight years later, presumably as owners. As a response to the legacy of slavery, these seem like defensible results.

Even in South Carolina, Reconstruction governance was something like making sausage—not pretty, but the dining wasn't that bad for the ex-slaves. Conservative rule offered freedmen little, but Republican leaders attended to their material needs, in public actions at least. Even inexperienced or less educated black lawmakers could perceive legislative betrayal and expose it. Besides, by the 1870s no one was calling legislators passive pawns, and the hostile reporter Edward King noted their "extraordinary aptitude" for parliamentary forms. In most legislatures the African-American presence was substantial, enabling representatives to push an egalitarian agenda with increasing effect. Desires for schools, farms, and social spending were costly—they raised taxes and facilitated corruption, but it is hard to fault the general direction of social policy. Using government for egalitarian change was the point of Republican rule, why freedmen risked their lives to vote, and it is unfortunate that malfeasance obscured the basic case. Moreover not all the Reconstruction reforms were expensive; lawmakers could rewrite the legal code to benefit those of modest means.

Take lien laws, the obscure provisions for who gets paid first in the event of debt proceedings. If a planter's crop failed, would his laborers be paid, or his other creditors? Widespread tenancy raised new issues, beginning with the legal status of sharecroppers: were they true tenants with the right to dispose of the crop, or just paid employees? It made considerable difference for who had the chance to cheat whom. The freedmen increasingly were "making their own purchases, and they sought for the cheapest dealers." If the landlord had priority, it would discourage anyone else from loaning money. Tenants would likely have to do business with the landlord himself or his preferred merchant. Given the high interest rates that characterized rural loans, this mattered. Mississippi's landlords complained they were dead last in the list of creditors, but Republican legislators somehow never corrected this situation. Only after Redemption were the laws rewritten entirely, to give landlords prior claim, to treat sharecroppers as employees, and even to take away the laborers' lien.

The legal system itself provided another avenue for racial change. Under Reconstruction most cities integrated their police forces, and the numbers of African Americans were substantial. In Mobile, not only did the police force contain a large black minority but many of them were described in the census as "black" rather than "mulatto," suggesting a democratizing impact. Once established, integrated police forces performed relatively well, and since property owners depended on police protection, they mostly accommodated the situation. Mobile's interracial police actually arrested a higher proportion of black suspects than their Presidential Reconstruction predecessors. In practice, urban areas saw large numbers of African Americans clothed with official authority, going about day-to-day tasks like anyone else. Similarly, in predominantly rural Mississippi, one-third of the freedpeople lived in plantation counties that had black sheriffs.

One study illustrates the legal transformation in Vicksburg, Mississippi, an area conspicuous for its African-American elected officials. According to Christopher Waldrep, blacks in Warren County comprised more than a third of all jurors, in several years more than half. The number remained below their proportion of the population but was always substantial. Republican officials sought black men with property, and in the early 1870s some 85 percent of black grand jurors said they could read and write. This bias toward respectability perhaps encouraged the high conviction rates. From 1868 to 1873 juries convicted a substantially higher percentage of black than white defendants, more than three-quarters, surely an effective rebuttal to claims of racial preference. Prosecutors actually won more often than they had previously, the exception being difficulty in convicting Republican officeholders accused of fraud. During this period racial access to the courts was transformed. African Americans were far more likely to press charges, both against whites and also against other blacks. A study of Republican-dominated Washington County, Texas, finds much the same pattern. The outcome approximates what modern observers might understand as racial justice. No legal process could satisfactorily replace slavery for most native whites, but it is striking that in these two Republican strongholds the formal legal system looks as democratic and functional as it does.

Reconstruction also transformed the terms of public discussion. Well over four hundred Republican newspapers appeared, a sizable proportion of the total in the ex-Confederate states. In South Carolina some twenty Republican newspapers were published in 1873, including three dailies. This press infrastructure furthered a bipartisan exchange, and for years a notably free press debated basic issues of governance. Moreover publicity could protect voters' lives, especially while Democratic papers were routinely promoting terrorism. The stakes were high. After a race riot the editor Albert Griffin was pursued by white mobs urged on by the *Mobile Register*. Repeated editorials called for Griffin's death, forcing him into exile. Such conduct made sense, for Republican publications threatened exposure to the outside world. Irked Democratic editors often damaged their cause with intemperate responses. During the Klan heyday the Republican press presence made the issue harder for Northerners to ignore.

As with many Reconstruction accomplishments, these gains came at considerable public cost. Since so much of the potential readership was illiterate, the prospects for profitable journalism were limited, and advertisers shunned Republican papers. One black speaker actually suggested that illiterates buy and keep copies of a Radical sheet as a legacy to succeeding generations— not an argument likely to win many subscribers. To survive, Republican newspapers required subsidies in the form of public printing. Under the spoils system these practices were normal, but the costs added to the financial pressures on Southern governments. Newspapers' need for funds also exacerbated Republican factional disputes. Still, given the later role of newspapers in whipping up racial extremism, this countervailing indigenous voice looks important, and it reinforced the literacy crusade. As one party publisher observed, freedpeople considered "every word published in a Republican paper almost law, and every paper taken on a plantation is better than a dozen speakers."

More broadly, it was in the political sphere that the achievements of Reconstruction were most apparent, in freedom of expression and participation. In the plantation belts the threat of violence often receded for years. Senator Adelbert Ames provided detailed discussions of life in politics to his wife. Despite occasional Klan scares and speaking affrays, Ames felt safe enough traveling about to run for governor of Mississippi in 1873, attending black social gatherings with gusto. He was invited to one get-together, and "Except as to color, nothing out of the usual order of a country ball was perceptible." On another occasion he addressed a group of African-American firemen, itself an indication of how much things had changed. When he dined at a black colleague's house, Ames was primarily impressed with the quality of the fare. The striking thing is how normal his politicking seems, save for his tendency toward three- and four-hour orations. Mississippi's leading carpetbagger apparently was secure enough on the stump for unhurried speeches.

African-American political participation became routine reality. Even white opponents got used to it, especially with respect to nonpartisan local votes, where Reconstruction tilted the electorate in favor of plantation neighborhoods. One Alabama planter noted the constant march of his employees to the polls on various referenda: "Carrs with music take the Negroes, Barbecue in Demopolis, Faunsdale, etc., etc." He regretted lost work time but otherwise voiced no complaints. A Mississippi planter witnessed a Republican speech and decided not to respond, knowing the freedmen would never be persuaded. A South Carolina farmer similarly observed, "Such things are abominable in the site of white men, but I suppose it must be endured." An unenlightened view, perhaps, but he wasn't reaching for his gun.

Demographic reality often encouraged accommodation. Francis Butler Leigh observed that while "everyone did the best he could for his party, there was not the least ill-feeling between the blacks and the whites and the election passed off without trouble of any sort, which is a noteworthy fact in itself." Of course the lopsided racial proportions in her Georgia low-country vicinity probably had something to do with it. Scholars generally conclude that Klan-style night riding was most common in areas with roughly equal numbers. If one assumes that a substantial black majority would inhibit Klan operations, large numbers of freedpeople lived in such circumstances. In Alabama, for example, 50.4 percent of the African-American population lived in counties with at least a two-thirds black majority, and in Mississippi the figure was 47.8 percent. South Carolina had 36.9 percent and Louisiana 36.1 percent—that is, well over a third of the black population. Counting just able-bodied men, the ratio would be higher given wartime losses. White paramilitaries might still prevail in open battle in such settings, given the disproportion in arms, horses, and military experience. But short of risking an outright firefight, terrorist intimidation was unlikely as a continuing reality.

Night-riding operations were difficult to sustain in many areas, and they often spent themselves after a year or two. The pattern was startlingly local: neighboring counties often had drastically different experiences. Furthermore Klan-style terrorism was never much in evidence in the Mississippi delta or the Louisiana sugar country after 1868, or in the Georgia and South Carolina low country. One South Carolina Republican recalled the uneven pattern: "While Negroes were as safe as anybody in the region of Columbia and Charleston, blood-curdling news from districts at a distance thrilled us now and again like tales of nearby Indian massacres." Virginia never experienced much of a Klan presence, and major cities were largely exempt. After the New Departure rhetoric became common, one finds a dispirited elite resignation to black suffrage across wide reaches of the plantation South.

Rural reality encouraged this political evolution: by the early 1870s former slaveholders were reconsidering the freedmen's work habits. With the stabilization of agricultural labor and good crop prices, compulsion seemed less essential. In 1870 both cotton and tobacco production reached per-acre postwar highs, according to government figures. In mid-1871 Horace Greeley talked to planters around Vicksburg who uniformly assured him "their ex-slaves are working better than they expected, and better this year than ever before." Greeley surmised they still preferred slavery, but the men at least were politic enough not to say so. Political grievances remained, overshadowing diminishing complaints about poor work habits. As sharecropping proved itself in practice, landowners accommodated a day-to-day reality that seemed increasingly functional.

Occasionally a more pragmatic mood found political expression, as in the 1873 "Unification" episode in Louisiana. After a disputed election and chaotic disorder, New Orleans businessmen spearheaded a campaign to meet black demands. With the aid of some of the disaffected Afro-Creole leadership, they sought a bipartisan reform movement. Led by ex-General Beauregard, the Unification leaders offered emphatic public support for civil rights provisions, including the integrated school system, if blacks would abandon the Republicans. Several declared their willingness to use their personal influence to encourage white compliance. The effort unraveled due to underlying black distrust; one black leader pointed out that there was time to talk about bipartisanship once assassination ceased. Still, hard-pressed community leaders went some lengths to accommodate civil rights demands, showing their discomfort with the harsh racial appeals other Democrats preferred.

What, then, is one to make of the overall social effect of Reconstruction? Wide sections of the South accommodated to the reality of legal equality. In his memoir of Reconstruction, Albert T. Morgan discerned egalitarian practices taking root across the Mississippi delta. After good crop prices in the late 1860s, freedmen were renting and even buying land for themselves. Yazoo City was swollen with small merchants seeking black customers, and by 1873 "it was boss and no longer [master], with many colored men." He even thought the freedmen had "improved very greatly in their manner of pronouncing English words." At a Republican county convention he noticed that nearly all the delegates could read, most could write, and three of the freedmen present were successful planters. Increasingly, blacks signed the property bonds so that Republicans could assume office. It was a gratifying pattern of change, ratified in his own case by marriage to a Northern schoolteacher of mixed ancestry. The social transformation, Morgan hoped, would stabilize everything the Radical Republicans had worked for. It was "simply a question of endurance," he thought, if they could "hold the fort a few years longer."

They couldn't. The national climate would change, and it would all be undone as completely as human ingenuity could devise. Still, Morgan wasn't dreaming; the trends he detailed were pervasive across much of the South. It was precisely because the transformation had been so substantial that the reaction was so abiding. Free schools, a free press, interracial juries, open access to public facilities, enthusiastic political participation—these were realities of the new regime. Given how much had changed, how much their world had been upended, it is not surprising that the mass of white Southerners resisted when they saw the opportunity. The tragedy is that circumstances soon allowed them to prevail through renewed violence, and that the national public let them do it.

8

The Politics of Slaughter: Depression and Reaction

MODERN HISTORIANS have generally paid more attention to the rising arc of Radical Reconstruction than its dispiriting conclusion. Eric Foner's commanding synthesis, *Reconstruction*, devotes just one hundred pages out of more than six hundred to the period after 1872. The eventual outcome, however, by no means looked foreordained. As one Republican noted, "You have but little idea how much my *respectability* has been increased by the [1872] election. . . . I am again recognized as a gentleman by the upper-tendom." The Liberal Republican misadventure solidified African-American influence over a unified majority party. Reasonable observers thought basic civil rights were guaranteed. As the *New York Times* observed, "Whatever wild hopes the Southerners may have entertained of modifying the result of the war, by unfriendly legislation or unfriendly administration, must be abandoned."

People assumed that ex-Confederate minorities would never be allowed to shoot their way into power. In four of the Deep South states—South Carolina, Mississippi, Louisiana, and Florida—the numbers promised continuing Republican influence, even dominance. In the 1872 elections Republicans regained ground elsewhere too. Even in the predominantly Democratic states, the threat of federal intervention inhibited exuberant racism. As long as Republicans controlled the White House and Congress—and thus the courts and the army—protection of voting rights would continue. Since African Americans remained so willing to pay the ongoing cost in lives, the Reconstruction settlement looked stable.

Circumstances appeared auspicious for a positive agenda, and the initiative shifted toward civil rights proponents. African-American leaders understood that certain concerns would not be pursued without pressure, and representation in elective office became one focus. In deference to Northern opinion, black leaders for some years pressed their claims cautiously. No African Americans had been among the initial forty-five Reconstruction congressmen, and none actually arrived in the House until 1870. White Republicans predominated in local office, even in overwhelmingly black counties. Officials handling funds required large property bonds, so landholders had a near veto power over the electorate. One Mississippi justice of the peace recalled that it was unthinkable to approach whites, and a black sheriff in Alabama lost his office when no property owner backed him. African Americans did better in legislative bodies, which had no such requirements, but in terms of constituent service and tangible appeal, local office mattered.

At first it seemed natural for experienced white Republicans to claim the offices, and they clung to them insistently. Officeholders were a clannish subculture, often clusters of relations relying on one another for moral support. Even the most polished black aspirants met sharp resistance from officeholders quick to discern a racial purge. Ironically the Radical Republican rhetoric of color-blind equality legitimized this pattern. Martin Delany pointed out that carpetbaggers employed arguments that Republicanism knew no race. The editor Philip Joseph similarly complained, "The white men in the Republican party fill all of the paying offices, and yet if a colored man dare part his lips on the subject he is charged with attempting to raise a black man's party." As black leaders sought the moral high ground, the churches furnished influential examples of a race-conscious approach. Confronting white denominational rivals, African Methodist Bishop Henry Turner supported the "help-yourself doctrine, which must ultimately triumph, if we ever triumph." Since ministers like Turner frequently went into politics, the logic of religious racial empowerment infused the electoral sphere.

The issue was ideological, but activists pursued it with redoubled zeal because they personally benefited. In late 1870 Frederick Douglass's *New National Era* defended racial preferences in government employment when candidates were equally qualified. Such nuances became less evident as African-American leaders pressed the issue. There was a democratic logic in these demands, and national opinion did not automatically respond negatively. When Hiram Revels won an interim term in the Senate from Mississippi, the press mostly applauded his assumption of Jefferson Davis's former seat. South Carolina's polished Congressman Robert Elliott received favorable publicity, even for good enunciation, as did his ex-slave colleague Robert Smalls, celebrated for wartime exploits. The fourteen black representatives and two senators who served during Reconstruction generally acquitted themselves well, both as spokesmen on racial issues and by dignified deportment. They punctured Southern Democratic assertions with great effect. These leaders also served as conduits of Washington reality to their constituents, a matter of urgency given what was happening back home.

The problematic issue occurred at more modest levels of government. African-American numbers in the legislatures grew, and these bodies already had established a dubious reputation. Also, the new legislators were less attuned to Northern sentiment than their worldly Washington counterparts. Still, by Grant's second term corruption was declining and retrenchment dominated the agenda. The change in local leadership was perhaps more crucial. As the 1870s proceeded, African Americans represented a growing proportion of lesser Republican officials. More than a hundred blacks served on county governing boards, along with some forty-one sheriffs. Of those county board members whose prewar status is known, about half were free while a disproportionate number appear to have had mixed ancestry. Relative to the mass of freedpeople, the social bias upward was pronounced. Executive officers mostly had substantial property and were overwhelmingly literate, but lesser officials looked different. Of more than fifteen hundred African Americans located at all levels of Reconstruction government, about two hundred were reported as illiterates in Eric Foner's exhaustive tabulation. In Mississippi, where only a tiny free black population existed before the war, former slaves were prominent on county-level governing boards. In the 1870s exactly half of these black officeholders of known background, seventeen of thirty-four, were reported as illiterate in Foner's count. A large majority had accumulated property before being elected to office, again marking them as successful relative to their constituents. Still, literacy was a minimal benchmark of competence in the eyes of the outside public.

An evident tension existed between the desire to promote qualified leadership and the choice of officials with typical experiences and interests. Even less learned officeholders could serve as community watchdogs, and education's connection with personal honesty is not all that evident. South Carolina's Governor Scott actually suggested electing farmers to office rather than former domestics with exposure to upper-class vices. Illiterates in minor offices may have served their constituents and justice better than available alternatives. Furthermore, one can discern surprising nuances of white opinion toward individual black officeholders. In Selma, Alabama, property holders put up the large bond for tax collector Benjamin Turner, a well-regarded former slave entrepreneur who was subsequently elected to Congress. One white leader wrote privately of Turner as polite and intelligent. Another resident conceded, "The negroes who hold office are sometimes preferable to the white men. The negro tax assessor of Dallas Co. & negro clerk to one of the courts . . . appear quite respectable, [but] the tax collector, a white man is drunk nearly all the time. . . ." Similarly, in black-dominated Natchez the generally critical reporter Edward King found that government seemed satisfactory. Officials appeared diligent, the schools looked fine, and even the children in the streets were getting along.

Black officeholding nonetheless sharpened the racial edge of Reconstruction. Direct representation had political drawbacks, given the prevalence-of-corruption discourse and its ready interplay with racial stereotypes. Disorderly finances during Reconstruction encouraged certain forms of local graft. Quasi-legal manipulation of warrants—paying off government IOUs favorably—was a widely reported practice. So was substituting depreciated warrants for cash to satisfy accounts. After leaving office, Louisiana's Governor Warmoth personally held $361,000 worth of state and local bonds, which suggests the prevalence of speculative opportunities. Although most malfeasance occurred before African Americans generally held local office, Democrats could claim extensive black involvement. These assertions are difficult to substantiate, given the often one-sided dominance of the press. What is clear is that government's composition changed in ways that could be portrayed badly before the public.

Whatever the political ramifications, the movement for popular representation met a grassroots response, which in some respects anticipated the 1960s "Black Power" movement. White officeholders had proven opportunistic or corrupt often enough to encourage this reaction. There was a rising rhetoric of popular rule and a less deferential attitude toward outside sensibilities in general. Ideologically, though, this movement differed from the movement of a century later because of the emphasis on integration—or at least equal access—in public places. Racial representation intersected with civil rights because this issue became the lever to displace entrenched white leaders. Republican officeholders generally resisted open-accommodations legislation on grounds of expediency or conviction. The situation invited challenge from energized activists on a matter of principle.

Black leaders also had insight into a social issue that others perceived less vividly. After emancipation, interracial contact in public became politicized, particularly in urban areas where the deferential behavior that whites expected became less prevalent. Evolving sidewalk etiquette generated numerous confrontations. Businesses often excluded African Americans or enforced separation. For instance, postwar streetcar companies commonly required African Americans to stand on outside platforms. Railroads normally required all blacks, men and women, to sit in the second-class or smoking car, and three states had mandated separation by law during Presidential Reconstruction. Restaurants and especially hotels raised a host of similar issues. The very profusion of anti-discrimination proposals highlights the prevalence of these practices. For the freedpeople, actual integration with whites was not the overriding goal, for segregated public schools were tacitly tolerated nearly everywhere. But discrimination in public spaces seemed different, an insulting badge of inferiority.

Internal political dynamics propelled escalating demands. Privileged African Americans often asserted initial leadership, only to be challenged by activists of a more popular profile. South Carolina's Martin Delany complained that among government appointees, almost all the African Americans had mixed ancestry. Faced with such internal criticism, what issue could better allow a beleaguered racial elite to assert leadership? Civil rights resonated with their own experience, legislators having extensive experience of hotels, restaurants, and public conveyances. The issue also offered a positive response for diffuse stirrings for change. One example illustrates the pattern. Mobile's Philip Joseph was a leading moderate spokesman. This scrupulously dressed Afro-Creole, from a slaveholding family, eventually lost his federal job and his following to popular rivals. Afterward Joseph recast himself as a journalistic civil rights advocate. A Democratic paper wondered what had happened, marveling that he "used to be rather a mild-mannered colored man." Joseph's situation propelled escalating demands, to the dismay of Republican officeholders who wished he would just go away.

Regulation of public accommodations was a long-accepted practice; even the hostile *Nation* initially supported the concept. Civil rights legislation cost little, which mattered given the diminishing prospects for government expenditure. In practice, once businesses found compliance necessary, matters generally sorted themselves out. Northern cities had already abandoned segregation on streetcars and railways. By 1874 all of New England had outlawed de jure segregation in schools. In view of the later development of Jim Crow, it is difficult to fault the logic of challenging these practices before they became entrenched. As some historians have pointed out, first-class accommodations became the focus, which suggested that a narrow constituency would benefit, especially Republican politicians themselves. Still, African Americans seldom raised this objection; few questioned that challenging patterns of exclusion helped the race as a whole. As the Alabama legislator William Councill observed, blacks favored civil rights legislation to a man.

The anti-discrimination provisions of Louisiana's constitution propelled the topic into its legislature and courts first, and

South Carolina soon followed. As black legislators became more experienced, they pressed for explicit laws with sufficient penalties to encourage compliance, and these became a flashpoint of factional controversy. In Mississippi, for example, a civil rights bill disappeared after passage in suspicious circumstances. At the national level, Senator Charles Sumner's stubborn promotion of the issue beginning in 1870 enhanced its profile. Frederick Douglass's paper hectored black politicians and Southern office-holders. After Grant's reelection, and his inaugural statement vaguely endorsing the concept, civil rights protections became a litmus test.

Knowing the eventual outcome of Reconstruction, these emphases may look misplaced, but in context both expanded office-holding and civil rights laws seemed reasonable. They made perfect sense if one assumed continued Republican dominance, and Grant's reelection was the closest thing to a landslide for decades. Republicans controlled Congress by huge margins. The Senate had forty-seven Republicans and seven Liberal Republicans, against just nineteen Democrats. The Fourteenth and Fifteenth Amendments were enshrined in the Constitution, and even the Democratic platform had conceded them as settled realities. Given the auspicious circumstances, pressing this last demand for public equality seemed right.

The flaw was that Northern support for Reconstruction did not exist in isolation. Federal protection was tied to other issues and the personal popularity of U. S. Grant. The Republican government that protected civil rights was also devoted to promotion of corporate enterprise. The Civil War was a watershed on tariff policy, banking legislation, transportation subsidies, and other growth measures. These policies were bound up with a vision of harmonious interests, articulated effectively by the ex-Whig Abraham Lincoln of log-cabin pedigree; economic progress would create a fluid social order open to upward mobility. The Northern middle and upper classes, especially Protestant churchgoers, embraced this vision, and they were the crucial Republican constituency, but even they were unsettled with the corporate flavor of the Grant administration. As the ideological passions of the war ebbed, the party machinery became more identified with industry and finance. Protected industry and subsidized railroads fared well, and so did bondholders, Union veterans, and other interest groups tied to the party. But Republican rule marginalized immigrants, the urban working class, and multitudes of Western farmers. Years of labor agitation, and in 1873 an emerging agrarian Grange movement, reflected their alienation.

Big money was in vogue in Republican Washington. The Credit Mobilier provided a vivid education in railroad political influence. Soon even the nation's most prominent anti-slavery preacher, Henry Ward Beecher, would be enmeshed in a spectacular sex scandal. Although the Liberal Republican revolt miscarried, its critique of widespread corruption remained influential. In 1872 most voters chose to "Stand Pat," in the words of a Republican campaign button, the poker metaphor nicely conveying Grant's image of masculine bonhomie. As long as the economy performed well, voters overlooked Grant's liabilities, but when economic circumstances soured, things changed quickly.

Railroads enjoyed premier billing in Gilded Age abuses, but the monetary issue rivaled their importance. During the Civil War, private currency chaos gave way to government greenbacks and regulated issue by nationally chartered banks under federal guidelines. Under the National Banking Acts, the supply of bank notes in circulation was tied to the size of the national debt, and after Appomattox the supply of greenbacks declined from wartime highs. Government policy thus kept the amount of currency relatively constant in a time of economic expansion. Deflation resulted, and those lending money, like bankers and bondholders, benefited since it insured payment in ever-stronger dollars. But debtors lost, especially farmers, because they borrowed money every year. The complexities took time to sink in, Jacksonian hard-money views being traditional among farmers, but Western discontent grew.

The banking community viewed things differently, of course. Northeastern financial leaders trusted Grant, though no one thought him personally acute on monetary issues. Bankers feared irresponsible tinkering, but the Republican financial system had inherent weaknesses. Every fall millions of dollars were shipped westward to pay for the crops, creating a credit crunch and depressing stock prices on Wall Street. Richard Bensel has argued that a seasonal currency shortage, exacerbated by government inaction, caused the September 1873 crash. If so, there is no evidence that federal officials perceived approaching disaster.

There was another problem. Railroads drove the Wall Street boom, and government aid policies encouraged speculation. In 1868 American railroad bonds worth $22 million were purchased in London; four years later bonds worth more than $100 million were bought. A bankers' publication concluded that European purchasers were indiscriminate, disproportionately investing in weaker lines. But foreign capital grew wary in view of bad publicity, leaving promoters exposed. In September 1873 Jay Cooke, a leading banker promoting a second transcontinental railroad, overextended himself and suspended payments. A panic ensued, and the subsequent collapse of the major broker of Southern bonds redoubled the damage. The stock exchange suspended activity for ten days, and a ruinous depression followed. Railroad construction declined from almost 7,500 miles in 1872 to 1,600 in 1875. Senator John Sherman observed, "The panic spread so that in a month all industries were in a measure suspended."

Five long years of economic decline ensued, and Grant privately called the depression a "disaster." The president settled on a back-to-basics response emphasizing sound money. He also called for tax increases and cutbacks to balance the budget. These actions had deflationary implications, and most historians think them counterproductive. The emphasis on specie resumption—a return to hard money as the basis for currency—seems especially ill-timed. As a Northern businessman observed, "There are earnest advocates of hard money who think his proposed treatment too drastic and heroic." Responding to demands for strong action, Congress in April 1874 passed what was termed an Inflation Bill. Experts questioned what the complicated measure would actually accomplish, but Grant feared concessions and vetoed the bill. His stand rallied dominant opinion in the hard-money Northeast behind him. Major journals rushed to his defense, but his position was less popular in the Midwest. Grant himself noted the general perception of "a triumph of Capital" over working people. Whatever the political fallout, the larger problem was that Grant's policies failed to relieve the depression. Anti-railroad third parties or coalitions swept the plains states, winning several legislatures, and ferocious labor violence broke out in the Pennsylvania coalfields, all this building toward the bloody national railroad strike of 1877. Fears of class war increasingly riveted the attention of the prosperous.

In the South, depression transformed the scene. The price of cotton declined by a third between 1872 and 1876 and then continued to fall. For years, profits had induced many whites to accommodate Reconstruction. Now disaster swept away all the hopeful habits of coexistence. One Alabama planter lost thousands on his 1873 crop, noting that there was nothing left to steal. He did not minimize the threat of starvation, he just steeled himself for a showdown. When sober means fail, confrontational solutions suggest themselves. Landowners blamed their tenants, emphasizing racial explanations for their woes. One newspaper complained that with the best plantations rented out, black

autonomy meant regional poverty. If planters were hurting, the
smaller farmers were even angrier, for their profit margin was
modest to begin with. Taxes threatened all landowners' economic survival, and vast quantities of land were forfeited. Previous divisions over secession and war seemed less urgent in the
face of this reality.

The rural crisis coincided with a sea change in the political
climate. The New Departure culminated in Greeley's defeat, and
the depressed South was soon littered with bankrupt railroads as
one state after another defaulted on its bond guarantees. Discretion had brought defeat, and Republicans suddenly looked so
weakened that an immoderate course might prevail. Democratic
small-government fundamentalism reemerged, combined with
hard-edged racial appeals. If conflict resulted, Democrats were
now less likely to be blamed. For Reconstruction to end in the
Republican states, blacks had to be kept from the polls forcibly,
given their disregard for economic pressure. Militants now
avowed this openly, for enforced discretion had become onerous.
The political issue was how this would play out before the nation.

A "straightout" Democratic campaign rejecting coalition
with Republican dissidents and highlighting racist violence materialized only gradually. Many hesitant whites, particularly in
the black belts, doubted that open extremism could succeed.
Louisiana became the proving ground, where insurrection began
even before the depression. The state was about the most violent
in the region, and it was never Reconstruction's showcase. Taxes
were more than twice the regional average in 1870, and government debt was by some measures the highest in the South. Governor Warmoth's long struggle with the customhouse faction
destabilized Republican rule. In this setting an unlikely string of
political events generated an explosion.

After the Klan-marred 1868 campaign carried the state
against Grant, the Republican legislature had determined on

drastic measures to protect black access to the ballot. It established a state "returning board" to certify election results. This allowed officeholders to void fraud but also allowed for partisan abuse. In the 1872 canvass the opposition "Fusionists" claimed victory, aided by Governor Warmoth's timely defection and his control of the registration machinery. Adroit maneuvers allowed Warmoth to purge the returning board with a claim of legality, and rival boards backed by court injunctions followed. The outgoing legislature impeached Warmoth, suspending him from office and making P. B. S. Pinchback acting governor. The Republican election board then declared winners, by estimate, without having secured physical access to the returns. Once again dual legislatures resulted, with opposing claimants for governor as well.

The outcome generated a sort of frustrated national distaste. Greeley's poor performance across the region makes a Republican victory in Louisiana plausible, though historians still puzzle over the outcome. Grant himself concluded, "The election was a gigantic fraud, and there are no reliable returns of its result." Having just won the presidential election, Republicans now perhaps worked too hard to save an evenly divided state. After a congressional subcommittee issued a report critical of the Republicans, Grant suggested a new election under national supervision. The Radical leader Benjamin Butler endorsed the idea. Congress could have established a precedent for direct federal monitoring of elections, which probably was the best chance for continuing protection of voting rights. Grant might have won some white acquiescence with an evident willingness to accept an adverse verdict. But congressional Republicans balked at such an incursion on traditional state prerogatives, potentially to benefit the opposition. It fell to the president to recognize a legal governor, and he chose the Republican William P. Kellogg, observing that his claim was as good as that of his fraud-tainted opponent.

Kellogg tried to tough things out, but conflict intensified. The Fusionists recognized their own government and attempted a takeover at the capitol, but Kellogg's biracial Metropolitan police arrested the leaders. In the countryside, though, a taxpayer boycott spread. Across northern Louisiana, Kellogg appointees attempted to assume local office, only to be turned out by armed whites. The process mostly proceeded without bloodshed, but some Republicans resisted. In April 1873, after provocative behavior on both sides, freedmen rallied to defend threatened officials at Colfax. Democrats besieged the Grant County courthouse and set the building on fire. After the freedmen surrendered, they were executed en masse. According to a federal judge, fifty-nine bodies were recovered, mostly with pistol wounds to the back of the head. The facts are not much in dispute, and other such episodes occurred. The following year six officeholders in Red River Parish were killed while in Democratic custody. The disorder again fixated the national press with Reconstruction chaos, undermining the appearance of a stable social order. As the *New York Times* asked in frustration, "Are there no Southern States but Louisiana?"

The state witnessed the most spectacular atrocities of the entire era. These were reckless measures, and some opponents of Reconstruction hesitated. After the Colfax massacre, the business community of New Orleans offered its "Unification" proposal, for even integrated schools and public places seemed better than chaos. Louisiana had always had a substantial cohort of organized white moderates, but when the depression hit that fall, circumstances changed. Voices of restraint went silent despite Governor Kellogg's personal probity and his cutting the property tax by a third. In 1874 insurgent politics coalesced in the form of an explicitly racist mass movement, the White Leagues. "Shall the white people of Louisiana govern Louisiana?" a resolution asked, and this open avowal set the tone. One Republican victim recalled a process of popular empowerment, with negotiators from the Democratic elite unable to control their followers.

The White Leagues became the Deep South model for regaining power. By abandoning the Klan's sheets, paramilitaries looked more like a legitimate political movement, with intimidation excused more readily as self-defense. The showdown came in September 1874 when Democratic leaders attempted yet another coup. White Leagues descended on New Orleans by the thousands, this time routing the Metropolitan police under General Longstreet at the foot of Canal Street. Grant sent troops, and the White Leagues immediately withdrew in an agile show of discretion. Grant thought this a winning issue, but the fall's elections became a snap referendum on Reconstruction in an unattractive venue. In *The Nation*'s view, the president enforced "the illegal orders of an incompetent court, in behalf of a local faction of which his brother-in-law was a leading member," and he recognized a governor whom a congressional committee had pronounced a usurper. An accumulation of half-truths, perhaps, but the Republicans had accumulated years of liabilities in Louisiana.

The national obligation nonetheless should have been clear: legal voters were being killed by racist mobs. There should have been some way to guarantee free elections while allowing flawed governments to be voted out. The federal government had crushed the Klan in recent memory, and terrorists almost never risked confronting the army, so the question is why the public lost patience now. In the century to come, Northerners never fully accepted the abridgment of suffrage rights, and the later civil rights movement would draw sustenance from this reality. But after the depression hit, it was hard to argue that Reconstruction had been a success or that further vigorous measures would bring order. Grant had been reelected on the strength of his pacification of the South, and now it was visibly unraveling.

Enforcement looked problematic elsewhere. Opposition fraud was so pervasive, and the consequence of defeat so dire, that Republicans often resorted to unattractive expedients. In 1873 Democrats swept Texas, and Governor Edmund J. Davis conceded their majority, but he sought to overturn the results on a technicality. Grant refused, but the situation in Arkansas underscored the perils of being drawn into state politics. After a disputed election victory in 1872, the presumably Radical Republican governor Elisha Baxter conciliated the opposition by reversing Arkansas's disfranchisement laws and disavowing an expensive railroad measure. His Liberal Republican opponent Joseph Brooks called upon regular Republicans to sustain his lengthy legal challenge, and after a favorable lower court decision in early 1874 his militias seized the statehouse. Black militiamen confusingly deployed on both sides, with casualties, though the army mostly kept the contenders apart. After some hesitation, Grant recognized Baxter, but a year later he again talked of installing Brooks to forestall a Democratic constitutional revision. The Brooks-Baxter war was easily lampooned, and it too raised the prospect of perpetual interference from Washington.

The depression was the real political problem, but Grant also made errors. When conciliatory Virginia conservatives improbably suggested another term for him, it reinforced misgivings over his use of the army. Avoidable talk of Caesarism was in the air. As the *Minneapolis Tribune* observed, the president's silence on a third term irritated the public. Southern Republicans were about the only enthusiastic third-term supporters, especially the freedpeople, which further distanced them from Northern opinion. Grant probably wanted another term, and perhaps he assumed his personal strength bolstered the Republican cause, but he misread public sentiment badly. It would take a subsequent drubbing in Northern local elections for him to disavow the idea.

The administration similarly blundered with respect to the justice system. Grant pardoned numbers of Klansmen early in his second term—precisely the wrong message. More fateful were his choices for four Supreme Court vacancies over his presidency along with numerous federal judges. He had difficulty finding candidates, especially in his second term, and he chose corporate conservatives like Joseph Bradley or relative unknowns like Chief Justice Morrison Waite. The president felt out their position on financial matters, but he neglected to take similar care with civil rights, even though journals like the *Independent* predicted the Court's future course. Lower court rulings looked ominous, and in the *Slaughter-House* cases (1873) the Supreme Court had construed the Fourteenth Amendment narrowly, imperiling the ability to punish political violence by individuals.

The long march toward *Plessy v. Ferguson* was under way, and administration leaders should have seen it coming. The 1875 *Reece* decision sapped the enforcement of the Fifteenth Amendment in state elections. In the *Cruikshank* case of 1876, the prosecution of the Colfax massacre, the Supreme Court concluded that the Fourteenth Amendment banned racial discrimination only by government. This undermined the Ku Klux laws, for if the states failed to act against individual violators, no earthly redress existed. The decision demonstrated that obviously guilty murderers could not be punished in federal court. It was a green light for racial extremism while providing a constitutional rationale for the retreat of Northern opinion. None of this had to happen. With lifetime tenure, the federal courts could have been a bastion of civil rights enforcement, but instead they orchestrated surrender. Given the fatal implications for his enforcement policies, Grant's inattention seems unaccountable.

Ultimately none of this may have mattered, given underlying Northern racial attitudes and the cooling passions of the war. Depression presidents seldom fare well at the ballot box. Still, there is the issue of how Southern Republicans presented themselves before the public. This is not a topic much emphasized in modern literature, which has tended toward rehabilitation of the Reconstruction governments, but it merits consideration. Republican leaders had acquired political liabilities that came due with the depression, and they were slow to respond. Given entire dependence on outside protection, it was incautious to rely too confidently on a local numerical majority anywhere. In South Carolina in particular, one can see long-standing defiance of national opinion, as in the case of Benjamin Whittemore, who was reelected to Congress after expulsion. The House barred him a second time, frustrated that his constituents thought his vending of West Point cadetships a small transgression.

Bribery became so routine that much of the political class was implicated, making it difficult later to clean house, for aspiring reformers were often outed. Governor Robert Scott won reelection and was succeeded in 1872 by the already implicated Franklin Moses, a former secessionist with an expansive lifestyle. Both men defeated all-Republican opposition tickets running on clean government pledges. With the implicit Democratic support for the dissidents, freedpeople naturally rallied to the regular Republicans. Still, tainted leadership left them vulnerable once the public mood soured. The legislature had corruption issues of its own. As one Republican recalled, "When I got there [in 1870] you could almost cut it with a knife. . . . It made one feel like going out and picking a pocket." One African-American visitor recalled staying in a rooming house filled with carousing representatives. It was too loud to sleep, and he lay in bed disconsolately pondering the implications.

Had Scott and especially Moses sought to undermine the reputation of Republican government, they could not have done a better job of it. As Moses later explained his popularity with the freedmen, "I flattered some, associated with others, but bought a great many more." The inconvenient fact was that in the state with the most pronounced African-American influence, corruption was pervasive, persistent, and widely publicized. Negative stereotypes abandoned, and James Pike's *The Prostrate State* galvanized a national outpouring. The *Atlantic Monthly* decried a sable despotism, resembling a "servile raid on the plantation henroost and smoke house." *The Nation* denounced "Socialism in South Carolina," seeing it as the symbol of the coddling of working people. The editors combined this class-drenched emphasis with crude racism. Average intelligence among low-country freedmen was "very low—so low that they are but slightly above the level of animals." Such statements in reputable Northern journals enormously encouraged Southern reaction. But the freedmen's limited education exacerbated the problem because it sheltered constituents from the hailstorm of national criticism.

Everywhere else corruption was in decline, but unfortunately for Republicans, South Carolina maintained its profile throughout the decisive year of 1874. Governor Moses sought renomination while under trial for purchasing a newspaper with state funds. *Harper's Weekly*, the largest mass-circulation journal, tallied 421 pardons by the governor, by category, illustrated with a Thomas Nast cover of Moses issuing armfuls to dubious-looking inmates. Another cartoon featured a dapper Moses and a convict standing over the broken Ten Commandments. The criticisms extended to the African-American leadership. The state's "ignorant and incompetent legislators" were depicted by yet another cartoon, this time a racial caricature of ranting black lawmakers. This was the behavior of a pro-Grant publication, which supported civil rights and enforcement measures. Republican editors flayed South Carolina to maintain any credibility before the Northern readership.

Eventually Grant had to respond. After a well-publicized taxpayers' convention, a delegation arrived pleading for intervention.

Grant testily pointed out that racial extremism had made matters worse, but he conceded, "I feel great sympathy with any people who are badly governed and overtaxed, as is the case in Louisiana, and as also seems to be the condition of South Carolina." This admission reflected political reality, and Grant privately warned Republicans that robbery had to stop. The state's congressional delegation urged against nomination of either Moses or Scott for governor. Congressman Robert Elliott had helped nominate Moses, but now he warned a crowd that "the colored people of South Carolina, are now on trial before the whole country." The eventual nominee, Daniel Chamberlain, vigorously pledged to clean house.

Louisiana and South Carolina explained much of the Democratic landslide to come. Historians frequently credit one other factor, the drive for federal civil rights legislation. If Reconstruction supporters still had a winning Southern issue, it was probably terrorism, and the civil rights proposal probably distracted the electorate unhelpfully. Still, it is difficult to determine how much it actually hurt in the North, given the accumulation of other Grant-era liabilities. The 1874 election postmortems didn't talk much about civil rights. At least the issue called to mind the party's idealistic origins rather than corruption and depression. Besides, it would have been difficult for national Republicans to evade the proposal. Senator Sumner had long promoted a federal ban on discrimination in schools, trains, and other public facilities. He earnestly believed this "final measure" for equal rights would make the freedpeople "comfortable & happy." With this encouragement from a respected ally, African-American congressmen made it their legislative priority. They were in position to testify personally for its necessity, for all had personal indignities to relate, showcasing black oratorical talent in the telling. One white Mississippi congressman conceded that they had responded effectively to Southern Democrats in debate. Sumner's demise in the spring of 1874, after a deathbed plea for passage, gave it an emotional impetus for anti-slavery veterans. The Senate passed the bill outright, but it stalled in committee in the House, which left it dangling before the electorate through the fall.

The proposal probably did more electoral harm in the South, especially the integrated school provision, though even here the question is complicated. To motivate black voters amid hard times and budget cuts, Republicans probably needed something positive. From Mississippi, Thomas Cardozo endorsed the civil rights proposal because previous gains had grown too stale to generate excitement. Only cataclysmic defeat would reorient black expectations drastically downward. Unfortunately the issue reinforced the White League strategy of racial polarization, especially in the states that still lacked such laws. Republicans representing scalawag constituencies, like Senator Brownlow, called the measure suicide, and poorer whites dependent on public education were particularly antagonized. Among Democrats, Northern criticism fed the sense that national sentiment had shifted, that things were finally moving in their direction.

White League–style mobilizations, by varied names, spread across the states in contention. Alabama illustrated the general trend. The state's scalawag-dominated government had balked on civil rights proposals, and the governor had renegotiated the state's railroad liabilities drastically downward. Governor David Lewis's personal honesty and deference to white sensitivities made no difference. Spontaneous armed bodies proliferated with lethal consequences. There was no safe response; freedmen could either cease political activities or mobilize for self-defense and risk a bloodbath.

Opponents also became much more adept at manipulating the press. In Sumter County a Republican speaker was killed and a black activist was shot off a train by armed bands. A Republican congressman published a letter alleging widespread terror, but it backfired when several claims could not be readily demonstrated. A *New York Tribune* reporter sent to the scene found nothing amiss, not with Union troops stationed nearby. A careful reading suggests reportorial hedging—this was the vicinity from which Klansmen had ridden the rails to the Meridian riot—and the reporter had evident doubts about white youths. No matter, the editors proclaimed Alabama nearly as peaceable as any state in the Union, and the paper preened itself editorially for years for its exposé. But Democrats didn't need universal terror to win close elections, just enough to tip the balance. That November, White Leaguers shot up a polling place at Eufaula. The *Tribune* blamed intimidation of black Democrats, a genuine issue everywhere in the South, but one which conveniently obscured the larger reality. The paper reported six whites and seventy-four blacks shot, at least ten fatally. A participant then published an anonymous letter apologizing for killing the son of a Republican judge, explaining that the judge himself had been the intended target. "We have more riots here than a little," one schoolboy later wrote. "We everlasting clear the negroes out."

Across the South the pattern was much the same. Republicans lost everywhere save for the three states where freedmen were most numerous, along with Mississippi which had no state elections. The decisive results, though, were in the North, for this was one of the great electoral reversals in American history. In the House, Republicans went from a 199-to-88 majority to a 106-to-183 minority, losing more than 90 seats. The scale was so huge that it retrospectively suggests inevitability. Democrats more than doubled their numbers overnight, and they would maintain their majority into the next decade. Holdovers assured Republicans of a diminished majority in the Senate, but still, as soon as the incoming Congress met, the legislative situation would be transformed.

In the South the Democratic response was glee: the end was in sight. The *Atlanta Constitution* described a political battleground "strewn with the fat sleek bodies of the slain." Republican atrocity mills had been "run to their full capacities," but the people could no longer be bamboozled. It was proven possible to intimidate black majorities without outraging Northerners. The practical implications were grave. Black self-defense measures had long functioned as the human tripwire for national intervention. Now the freedpeople were on their own, at least until the public temper changed or something truly horrific happened. In the plantation belt this transformed everything, for legions of Confederate veterans suddenly could exploit their paramilitary advantages without restraint.

The Grant administration scrambled to prevent the worst. It was becoming evident that once Democrats regained power, measures like Georgia's poll tax could deter voting without directly violating the Fifteenth Amendment, especially without a Republican Congress poised to intervene. Alabama's 1875 constitution would halve black voting, primarily by requiring that ballots be cast in home precincts rather than at county seats where there were plenty of witnesses. Grant himself spoke of preserving public education and basic rights from constitutional revision, but limited time made the legislative options few. Everything changed once Republican politicians realized the South was no longer a winning issue. Most Northern Congressmen sought to rein in the party's commitments, because the most expedient interpretation of defeat blamed Reconstruction rather than the rest of the party's policies. And yet another disputed outcome in Louisiana, with yet another military intervention to break up a Democratic seizure of the legislature, intensified this reaction. Union General Philip Sheridan recommended drumhead trials of Democratic "banditti," but the press blasted him and also the administration. As Congressman James

Garfield privately observed, the Louisiana millstone threatened "to sink our party out of sight."

Whatever could be salvaged legislatively would have to be done hurriedly by the lame-duck Congress. There were two major proposals, the civil rights act and a "Force Bill," reauthorizing martial law and federal monitoring of the polls. Curiously, it was the stalled civil rights bill that gathered steam. In debate, Southern Democrats offended congressional decorum through personal insults to black colleagues. Angry Republicans rallied, passing a civil rights bill stripped of its school integration provision, with five hundred dollars in damages to victims as the primary enforcement mechanism. The companion Force Bill failed. When a black colleague asked James G. Blaine why, the majority leader said that if the bill had passed, Republican defeat was a foregone conclusion. A presidential election was coming, and candidate Blaine thought that "if we saved the North we could then look after the South."

If salvaging Reconstruction was still possible, the priority of the two bills was arguably wrong. A force bill could have bolstered Grant's authority, which would have helped in Mississippi's coming election; it might also have encouraged the courts to sustain enforcement. Federal oversight would have put more outside witnesses at the polling places. The national press opposed the bill, but elections were still months away. Most Northerners felt ambivalent about abandoning the freedmen, and they distrusted the resurgent Democrats on the race issue, so there was some prospect for turning the debate around. As Grant pointed out with effect, "Fierce denunciations ring through the country about office-holding and election matters in Louisiana, while every one of the Colfax miscreants goes unwhipped of justice." It was true, and Northerners might yet do something about it. Unfortunately the new dynamic pushed Southern Republicans into ever more dangerous situations, to provide more obvious justifications for federal intervention.

A continuing string of scandals diminished Grant's political capital, weakening his ability to intervene. His friend Orville Babcock was implicated in the Whiskey Ring fraud; the presidential aide was apparently feeding inside information to federal officials who were bilking the government out of millions. The president cooperated little in the prosecutions, and perhaps obstructed them. Two cabinet members also would resign under charges of corruption. Amid all these woes, and the continuing depression, Republicans sought to change the subject, and Catholic influence became a topic of choice. Hostility to Irish immigrants was a long tradition among Republican voters, now inflamed by church demands for influence over education and aid for parochial schools. Thomas Nast's cartoons, for example, gave Irish Americans an anthropoid look; he depicted mitred bishops as crocodiles menacing schoolchildren. The problem was that for such alternative issues to work, Grant had to avoid Southern interventions.

The Mississippi legislative elections played out in this unpromising context. If Republican rule and voting rights enforcement had a success story, Mississippi was it. Adelbert Ames had been elected governor in 1873 over ex-Governor Alcorn, but with some white acquiescence because of promises of fiscal restraint. Ames did what he could, lowering tax rates slightly and vetoing suspect railroad bills, but unlike Governor Chamberlain in South Carolina, or even Kellogg in Louisiana, he did not push retrenchment to the point of antagonizing black legislators. Nor did he act as aggressively against local malfeasance, and there would be embarrassing issues in his administration, some involving African-American officials. Lieutenant Governor A. K. Davis would be indicted for selling pardons, and Ames thought him probably guilty. The superintendent of education, Thomas Cardozo, would also later be tried on theft charges. Democrats felt betrayed, and the White League campaign in neighboring Louisiana roused them to action.

A riot in Vicksburg became the focus of national attention soon after the Democratic congressional triumph. As was often the case, the origins were complicated. Because Mississippi's state government mostly avoided railroad subsidies, local governments pursued them, generally with bipartisan support. Heavy taxes for now-failing projects, and a local tradition of warrant manipulation, encouraged racial extremism. The *Daily Vicksburger* boasted that it was among the first Southern newspapers to advocate the Color Line. In 1873 the Republican electorate replaced corrupt white officials with equally culpable black ones. Several were later indicted, but a jury refused to convict in circumstances resembling racist insurrection. Armed whites then won possession of city government, and in December 1874 the taxpayers league went after Sheriff Peter Crosby, who later proved to have his accounts in order. Taxpayers challenged his official bond, and a mob forced his resignation. Crosby then went to Governor Ames, who, having feared to mobilize the militia, told him to gather a posse to retake his office. Sheriff Crosby's loosely worded proclamation prompted hundreds of supporters to march to Vicksburg. It looked like race war, and even white Republicans turned out to defend the town.

When the contending forces met on the old battlefield, Sheriff Crosby's followers turned back. As they withdrew, it appears whites armed with longer-range rifles began picking them off. A one-sided battle ensued, and horsemen pursued freedmen through the countryside for days. Vicksburg's mayor conceded sixty to eighty freedmen killed. The Democratic version, disseminated through the Associated Press, fooled few. The *Chicago Tribune* cynically commented on the initial tales of black atrocities, which evaporated upon inspection. The *Boston Globe* similarly scoffed at the usual report of scores of blacks killed and one white man severely wounded. The body count was too lopsided to disguise reality for long, but now Northerners drew different conclusions. The Republican *New York Times* thought the riot demonstrated "how weak all negro governments are, and what a few determined white men can accomplish."

Vicksburg formed the backdrop for a violent fall campaign. Governor Ames faced insurrection, but Republican papers decried pleas for troops. As Ames wrote his wife, "All the sins and iniquities of Republican rule in South Carolina, Louisiana, and other Republican states are weighed against me in judgement of the country." The emerging political reality was that now it took corpses to cover a vigorous response, and Washington wanted Republicans to defend themselves. If the militia was resisted, why, then, troops could come. But Mississippi's militia would be nearly all black, a situation promising yet more carnage. The governor held off until a riot outside Jackson, where a rally was disrupted by gunfire followed by another mounted manhunt. Ames then gingerly deployed a few militia units. In Yazoo County, near Vicksburg, Ames offered to restore deposed Sheriff Albert Morgan, but the sheriff refused, fearing for his life.

In September 1875 Ames officially called on the president to send soldiers. The legal obligation was clear, but with Northern state elections looming, Grant temporized. "The whole public are tired out with these annual, autumnal outbreaks in the South," he complained. Besides, he thought, the press lied so badly that the vast majority would condemn any interference. Grant nonetheless approved the governor's request, but his attorney general, Edwards Pierrepont, resisted his indecisive assent. Pierrepont did not think the Constitution authorized sending troops where the government was upheld by a great majority. Republicans instead needed "the manhood to *fight* for their rights and destroy the bloody ruffians." Ames got plentiful advice to show pluck, and even his wife suggested that a race war might be just what whites deserved.

Ames was in an impossible situation. The former general believed his "Negro militia has not the courage or nerve—whatever it may be called—to act the part of soldiers." But a certain lack of martial enthusiasm seems reasonable, for freedmen had seen the probable results. As for the Democrats, some leaders now believed they would win as things stood and talked of concessions. Through a federal mediator, they promised a truce if militia deployment ceased. The situation worked out perfectly for them, because when agreement broke down after some days, troops arrived too late for a campaign. Ames finally told voters to stay home, which prevented most election-day violence, though there was another riot a few days afterward. Republican votes in Yazoo County fell from three thousand to seven. Statewide the Democratic majority was thirty thousand, and the party took control of the legislature and forced Ames's resignation. He blamed the freedmen for their timidity, but he knew the real responsibility lay elsewhere, with Washington and the North. "The political death of the Negro will forever release the nation from the weariness from such 'political outbreaks,'" he sadly concluded.

Grant characterized the situation as a choice between Mississippi and Ohio. He may have been right, but he probably made the wrong choice. The Mississippi loss was irreversible, forcing the brokered presidential outcome of the following year. The outcome also guaranteed that in 1876 the Reconstruction debates would feature less attractive venues, like Louisiana and South Carolina. But the off-year Northern elections did show Republican gains, especially in Ohio where Rutherford B. Hayes was narrowly elected governor on the anti-Catholic and sound-money issues. Opportunism was in evidence, but some Republicans hoped to regain their footing so that basic civil rights protection could continue. Grant certainly viewed his policies in this light, and he imaginatively linked these issues rhetorically. He urged voters to "Encourage free schools [in the South] and resolve that not one dollar of money . . . shall be appropriated to the support of any sectarian school." But whatever the intention, most Northern observers now saw "home rule" as inevitable, and given the state of national opinion, it probably was. The coming presidential election campaign would determine how this sad outcome would be accomplished and how far the reaction would go.

9

Endgame in South Carolina: 1877 and After

BY THE MID-1870s Northern opinion had turned against Reconstruction like a strong wind. The *Atlantic Monthly* published a visitor's happy account of interregional reconciliation in the Deep South without even broaching the issue of racial attitudes. *The Nation* worked up more outrage over the expulsion of an alleged atheist from the North Carolina legislature than continuing violence. The once-Radical *New York Tribune* approached self-parody: "The South was so long a conquered province, ruled by the Attorney-General's quill and held in place with the bayonets of the army, that it is hard to realize that it is free at last." In this climate, given the imbalance now in force, the likelihood was that the remaining Reconstruction governments would be overthrown. And Democrats had devised the techniques to perpetuate their power, without prompting court interference or Northern outrage, once they gained even momentary control.

Deliverance was sure to come before long, *The Nation* assured white Louisianans, and there was probably little Southern Republicans could do about it. In both Louisiana and Florida, Republicans no longer controlled both houses of the legislature, so they were in no position to pursue reforms too vigorously. Governors could, and did, cut budgets and taxes, but these incre-

mental measures were not about to transform Northern percep-
tions of, say, Louisiana Republicans. There was, however, one
last desperate attempt to salvage the reputation of Republican
Reconstruction, partially at black initiative. The situation in
South Carolina was altogether unique, with its large Republican
majority and status as moral pincushion. The *New York Times*
termed Franklin Moses the "Robber Governor," but he was also
identified with popular rule, and it took much persuasion by
black leaders to uproot him. But subsequent events proved the
freedpeople could not stand the political dismemberment that
national sentiment demanded.

South Carolina's former attorney general Daniel Chamberlain would be the agent of respectable reform. Originally from
Massachusetts, Chamberlain had abolitionist ties and had volun-
teered for service with African-American troops. In some respects, though, he was an odd choice as a reformer, because he
had been involved in suspect episodes. He had been on the state
land commission, perhaps receiving kickbacks. He also had been
on the oversight committee for the state's issuance of bonds, and
had even gotten his college classmate, H. H. Kimpton, a job as
the state's fiscal agent. During the railroad aid heyday, he had
purchased a bankrupt state-held railroad in partnership with
other Republican politicians, in an attempt to consolidate it with
other troubled roads. As Chamberlain once wrote Kimpton,
"There is a *mint* of money in this or I am a fool. . . . There is an
infinite verge for expansion of power before us." He was dead
wrong, as it turned out, but the intent was clear enough.

Still, by South Carolina standards, these were moderate failings, and Chamberlain discreetly withdrew into private law
practice when Governor Moses assumed office. He was conveniently situated when Republicans sought a different profile.
Chamberlain would win election as governor in 1874 over an independent Republican running with Democratic support. The

national reverses encouraged a fresh approach, and he warned lawmakers that the eyes of the nation were on their state. Perhaps Chamberlain's own spotted past gave him something to prove, but whatever his personal calculations, conciliating the Democrats demanded addressing their sense of grievance. Chamberlain's inaugural address proclaimed reform priorities: to repair the state's tattered credit, and to cut taxes and assessments. More strikingly, he denounced widespread incompetence among local officeholders, accusing school officials of lax work habits. He also called the state's local trial judges, often appointed by Moses, generally deficient. He later claimed that more than half were illiterate, and he would appoint conservatives to some of these positions. Chamberlain's criticism had unsettling racial implications, and Democrats more than stunned Republican legislators applauded the speech. As the black journalist Richard Greener observed, "The message seemed to concede almost all the Conservatives had said, and resembled somewhat a Jeremiad." Greener perceived that even well-meant reform involved stripping power from black hands.

Shock therapy for Republican loyalists ensued. Chamberlain prevented a circuit judgeship for William Whipper, a well-connected black legislator with some legal experience. Chamberlain publicly charged him with embezzlement. After a tumultuous meeting the governor's supporters, aided by the Democrats, instead appointed a moderate white Republican. This was a difficult outcome for the Republican leadership; while Whipper gambled flamboyantly, and historians think he took bribes, he had never been convicted. As Whipper himself pointed out, Attorney General Chamberlain had never charged him with anything. The broader concern was that Whipper had been sacrificed to demonstrate the governor's rectitude.

Chamberlain's spending priorities provided other grounds for discontent. Tax revenues were well below expenditures, and borrowing money was impossible. Chamberlain did maintain funding for the public schools, and the number of students increased throughout his term. He also favored reopening the institution for the deaf, dumb, and blind. But otherwise he favored drastic cutbacks: to the lunatic asylum, the orphan asylum, and the state university now integrated by aspiring legislators. He decimated the public printing appropriation, wiping out the Republican press. Chamberlain also favored some sort of guaranteed minority white representation, through cumulative voting or other means. Beyond this the governor sought large property tax reductions, on the order of one-third, at a time when his depression-struck constituents sought public aid.

The tone of political discourse also shifted. Chamberlain's rhetoric suggested that the freedpeople's misdeeds, rather than white racists, were South Carolina's outstanding public problem. The emphasis on corruption shifted the spotlight from issues that were arguably more urgent. Chamberlain could have denounced political violence in his inaugural address, one Democratic paper observed, but "with commendable good taste, he makes not the slightest allusion to these exciting topics." When Democrats talked of bipartisanship and good government, African Americans saw terrorists in the wings—with justification, as it turned out. Chamberlain depicted his Republican opposition as motivated by personal gain, but there were real political concerns, and it is difficult to determine the weight of the various motivations. Perhaps the judicious conclusion is that a combination of personal interest, partisan and racial solidarity, and constituents' needs encouraged the Republican resistance.

If Chamberlain sought to reshape public opinion toward Reconstruction, it worked, but primarily for him personally. Praise from Southern Democrats and the national press were mutually reinforcing. Northerners rejoiced in a reforming Yankee governor who actually gained elite support. Even the state's leading

Democratic paper, the *Charleston News and Courier*, noted the outpouring of national admiration, and most local papers joined in the praise. Many Democrats were so shell-shocked they expediently welcomed aid from any quarter, and they also calculated that Chamberlain was disrupting the opposition. With Democratic help, and that of an interracial cohort of reform Republicans, the governor gained a measure of legislative influence. He had numerous vetoes sustained against the Republican majority. He also presided over drastic reductions in taxation rates and state expenditures.

For black leaders these were not reassuring trends. The governor refurbished his reputation at the cost of demonizing his Republican allies and democratic governance in general. The racial animus of the national praise for Chamberlain was difficult to miss. The *Boston Advertiser* observed that theft was not one of anyone's civil rights. The *Chicago Tribune* declared, "It is time that the negroes who have been disgracing their race, themselves, and American institutions by their reckless venality should learn that stealing must stop somewhere." *The Nation* derided legislation by barbers, porters, and caterers, praising the governor for his defense of civilization against barbarism. The racial characterization embittered Republican loyalists, making normal legislative give-and-take difficult.

Chamberlain's former sponsors bristled at being the foils of his public relations campaign. Whatever their failings, South Carolina's black leadership was composed of alert, experienced politicians who believed in racial equality. Pike's *Prostrate State* observed: "They have a genuine interest and a genuine earnestness in the business of the assembly," which was about the sole virtue he conceded them. Such men did not relish criticism emanating from a white politician with a checkered past, and had they been privy to Chamberlain's correspondence, they would not have been reassured. He and Democratic editors conferred warmly over outwitting his Republican critics. He shared many of the Democrats' negative beliefs about local governance. Decades later he reflected that "good government, or even tolerable administration, could not be had from such an aggregation of ignorance and inexperience. . . ." Furthermore Democratic leaders promoted social contacts for the Yale-educated governor and his wife, "lately a great belle in Washington society." The governor spoke at the Charleston Chamber of Commerce, private colleges, and other elite venues. Unlike his predecessors, Chamberlain could hardly socialize with black legislators while seeking such favors. Being accepted as a gentleman meant drawing the color line, and Chamberlain himself conceded that his desire for social recognition had become a political issue.

When Republicans suspected Chamberlain might jump ship, their frustration found expression in an early impeachment effort against the governor's closest black ally. State Treasurer Francis Cardozo disallowed numerous suspect claims, which probably motivated some of the hostility. Still, there were other resentments against the well-heeled Cardozo, the college-educated son of a planter, who led a faction of mostly freeborn, urban, mixed-ancestry supporters. Rural ex-slaves dominated his legislative opposition, and this factional lineup appeared on other issues. Overall, black Republicans probably should have submitted to the gubernatorial browbeating; their reputation was so poor that their obstruction backfired, and Northern support would soon become a matter of life and death. But legislators would be pushed only so far on painful measures to conciliate hated foes and satisfy distant opinion. Late in 1875 opponents took advantage of Chamberlain's absence for a college address to engineer a vote of no confidence. House Speaker Elliott scheduled a vote for circuit judges, and among those chosen were both William Whipper and former governor Moses himself. As one Republican explained what had happened, "The Governor, instead of talking to his friends . . . saw fit to use the goad and lash upon the party from the time he came into power until now, and he used that goad once too often, and that is the reason why [Moses and Whipper] were elected."

Here was an eye-catching challenge to the governor's leadership, in time for the presidential nomination season. Perhaps parliamentary tactics determined the issue: "Here's something Chamberlain can't veto," legislators reportedly observed. Constituent pressure must have been strong, because ex-Congressman Elliott and his colleagues likely anticipated the national reaction. Several journals thought the episode justified the Mississippi outrage and undermined the freedmen's cause. Thus bolstered, Chamberlain found a technical excuse to avoid commissioning the judges, and the *New York Times* thought his dubious position politically impregnable. The press outcry belatedly intimidated legislators, and Chamberlain faced down his critics at a heated Republican convention the following spring.

From the grassroots perspective, however, there were compensations. The Republican revolt undermined Chamberlain's bipartisan balancing act by reminding Democrats anew of how much they loathed Reconstruction. As one Charleston speaker warned, "You must make a good government, or they will make a Hayti." Outrage emboldened opponents to contest the next election under the Democratic label for the first time in years. Moreover national Democrats were criticizing the local détente with the governor. The *New York World*, for example, pointed to the Mississippi plan and suggested that South Carolinians could "by a similar course, achieve the same success." The implication, given the huge Republican majority, was a campaign of racial intimidation. Democrats divided bitterly over whether this was a viable response to the state's unique demographics.

This was the situation as the presidential campaign of 1876 took shape, in which South Carolina would pay a decisive role.

Although the Republicans nationally had recovered somewhat from the 1874 landslide, the depression showed no sign of lifting. Republicans would need the three Southern states they still controlled—and knew they had little chance in the rest. The party tried to shed President Grant's varied liabilities. That summer Republicans nominated Governor Rutherford B. Hayes of Ohio. The Democrats, for their part, nominated Governor Samuel Tilden of New York, who had led the prosecution of the Tweed Ring. Both candidates had credentials as clean-government reformers; both were hard-money diehards who appealed to independents less responsive to the old sectional issues. But Southern events, one way or the other, were to be important as the election heated up.

In both Florida and Louisiana, black numbers were not as great, and Democrats hoped for victory without risking a national backlash. The repeated deployment of federal troops in Louisiana also dampened down violence. All this focused attention on South Carolina, and the Democratic alliance with Governor Chamberlain raised tactical issues. Some pragmatists suggested that state Democrats let the national ticket take care of itself. As the *Charleston News and Courier* observed, "With Mr. Chamberlain as Governor, and a Conservative Democratic majority, or thereabouts, in the lower House, the State, in every sense of the word, would be safe. In attempting to gain more we might lose every thing." Power might well fall into Democratic hands in due course with little additional turmoil. Away from the overwhelmingly black low country, though, a "Straightout" mobilization along White League lines inspired more enthusiasm.

A major racial outbreak resolved the issue—at Hamburg, just across the Savannah River from Augusta. Reconstruction governance in this overwhelmingly black locality provided one grievance. The governor noted white reports that "the funds of the county are now being squandered on the poor, while the roads, bridges, and other great interests of the county are almost wholly neglected." Chamberlain rather endorsed the complaints, but his characterization suggests that policy preferences rather than corruption were the issue. After episodes of violence and arson on both sides, freedmen remobilized the long-dormant state militia, and a murder followed by the lynching of five black suspects intensified racial tension. On the Fourth of July, parading militiamen blocked a passing carriage, and words were exchanged. The Democratic politician M. C. Butler then prosecuted the militiamen for obstructing the public road. The intimidated black trial judge found the defiant commander in contempt, and the freedmen defensively barricaded themselves. Butler sought white reinforcements from Augusta, and when his deadline to disarm passed, he ordered an assault, complete with cannon. After the defenders surrendered, the leaders were told to run, then shot down. One white and seven blacks died in all, including the town marshal, whose body was mutilated. Several more freedmen were badly wounded.

Republicans rained criticism on the rioters, building electoral support with yet another ex-Rebel atrocity. Even the Democratic press was surprisingly critical. An Augusta paper initially suggested that Butler (soon to be elected U.S. senator) had been hasty. The *Atlanta Constitution* found "no evidence that the negroes intended bloodshed, opened hostilities, or could not have been induced" to surrender their arms. A subsequent riot in nearby Ellenton reemphasized the gravity of the situation. Northern papers urged resolute measures upon Governor Chamberlain, who was shocked at the behavior of his late admirers. His national reputation redoubled the impact of his denunciation. He called for federal troops, which President Grant sent after weeks of hesitation. Soldiers deployed through the state with orders to disband the rifle clubs. Whites felt betrayed, and bipartisanship unraveled: Chamberlain soon found himself on a Republican ticket with men he had recently denounced as scoundrels. As one black speaker assured a skeptical crowd, Chamberlain "was a straight-out Radical now, and such a policy as coalition had been killed beyond hope of recovery." Even so, hard-line Democrats only narrowly prevailed at the state convention, and perhaps only a confrontational strike among low-country rice workers clinched the outcome.

Ex-Confederate General Wade Hampton, the Democratic nominee, conciliated moderates with reassuring talk, but his straightout sponsors knew the score. In the papers of Martin Gary there exists a campaign plan for Edgefield County, nearby the recent outbreaks, which in more discreet form circulated throughout the state. Military clubs were to attend all Republican meetings and demand speaking time: "Democrats must go in as large numbers as they can get together, and well armed . . . and so soon as their leaders or speakers begin to speak and make false statements of facts, tell them *then* and *there* to their faces, that they are liars, thieves and Rascals. . . . If you get a chance get upon the Platform and address the negroes."

The Edgefield directive was startlingly explicit. "Never threaten a man individually," the document urged. "If he deserves to be threatened, the necessities of the times require that he *should die*." Gary's private jottings were still more sanguinary, and politics proceeded by his script. When the governor addressed a rally at Edgefield courthouse, Democrats muscled their way to the front of the crowd and even onto the speakers' stand. All were "heavily armed with pistols, displayed in many instances on the front of their persons, or even in their hands." Hecklers challenged him, and Chamberlain understood his life to be in danger. Generals Butler and Gary responded with personal abuse, and when the governor departed, armed whites entered his train car and warned him not to return.

Paramilitary organizations, called Red Shirts, accompanied Hampton across the state. The mobilization galvanized enthusiasm and also coerced participation from reluctant whites. Chamberlain counted 213 rifle clubs, with over 13,000 men, mostly armed with recently purchased rapid-fire rifles. As he pointed out, reorganizing the militia in response was suicidal, but the arrival of federal forces in October changed the situation. When troops arrived in Edgefield it seemed "the poor people would go wild with joy," with freedmen taunting the departing Red Shirts. Afterward confrontations became less one-sided, at least in the low country. At Cainhoy, outside Charleston, the freedpeople prevailed against outnumbered whites attending a Republican rally, killing several. Another white was killed in a similar confrontation in Charleston. Chaos continued, somewhat mitigated by the Democrats' fears of national repercussions, and election day itself was relatively quiet.

The presidential election of 1876 yielded a disputed national outcome. The Democratic candidate carried the reported popular vote, his numbers swollen by the already Redeemed states. Tilden won an undisputed 184 electoral votes, one short of a majority, with the votes of the three remaining Republican states in dispute (along with a contested elector in Oregon). But returning boards in all three could certify Republican majorities, making them on their face the legal results. Lawyers headed southward, and money was deployed plentifully. In both Louisiana and Florida, Republican state officials sustained Hayes, which left the results in South Carolina decisive. Initial returns showed both Tilden and Hampton with a narrow majority, though there were pervasive complaints on both sides. The Democrats claimed a three-thousand-vote majority in Edgefield County, even though blacks comprised the majority and Hampton's vote exceeded the total adult male population. The state returning board threw out the returns in Edgefield and one other black-majority county, declaring both Hayes and Chamberlain victorious.

A national uproar resulted, and all sorts of scenarios came into play, the constitutional procedures being indistinct on such matters. If the Democraic majority in the House obstructed the final count, by filibuster or otherwise, the army's position became relevant. Another civil war seemed possible, Lincoln's election having prompted the last one. Congressional Republicans backed off from the more confrontational options, and with President Grant's endorsement, Congress approved an extra-constitutional commission to determine the outcome. It then transpired that the Republicans, somewhat fortuitously, controlled this electoral commission. The Republican majority refused to go behind the official returns, making Hayes the winner.

While these events transpired, events hung fire in the three disputed Southern states. By this point Democrats had refined their manipulation of national opinion; it was far easier to install a contesting regime than to overthrow a recognized government outright. This became the pattern in all three disputed states, though in Florida a state supreme court decision gave Democrats control. In South Carolina, under army protection, Republican legislators barred Edgefield County claimants, whereupon the Democrats organized their own rival legislature. Both met in the legislative chambers, with the army keeping order. Chamberlain and Hampton both claimed election as governor, a situation ripe with potential bloodshed. Hampton reportedly warned Elliott, "If I were now to take my hands off the brakes for an hour, [Chamberlain's] life would not be safe."

More troubling for Chamberlain, though, were rumors from Washington. With the national outcome resolved, President-elect Hayes no longer needed Southern Republicans. By this point even President Grant acquiesced in what seemed inevitable. Just before leaving office, he ordered the army to cease protecting the Louisiana government, a revealing decision for a leader so identified with civil rights enforcement. In his diary Hayes had written of the need for a new direction in the South, and the disputed outcome only reinforced this inclination. Republican negotiators closeted with Southern Democrats to ease assumption of the presidency. The specific terms are still under contention, but Hayes's intimates clearly indicated that military protection would cease. Hayes actually delayed Grant's withdrawal order, seeking a peaceful transition and assurances that black rights would somehow be protected.

In the case of South Carolina, the new policy meant abandonment of a majority government and of a chief executive with strong credentials as a reformer. The outcome demonstrates the state of public sentiment, for everyone knew terrorists had prevailed. Chamberlain was called to Washington to hear the verdict, and he talked of continued resistance, but even the black leadership warned him to desist. Chamberlain departed with the words, "Today—April 10, 1877—by the order of the President whom your votes alone rescued from overwhelming defeat, the Government of the United States abandons you . . . with the full knowledge that the lawful Government of the State will be speedily overthrown. . . ." Two weeks later Hayes ended protection of Governor Kellogg in Louisiana, sending the troops back to their barracks, and so Reconstruction came to a deceptively peaceful end.

Historians have long criticized Rutherford B. Hayes for a culminating betrayal of civil rights. The incoming president's course was politically expedient, and the decades after "Home Rule" were certainly dire enough. But who was to blame, President Hayes or Northern sentiment in general? Even Grant thought the end had come, at least in Louisiana. All the pragmatic arguments favored the racists. As *The Nation* observed, "It is only in the states that the negroes are actually governing . . .

that the whites give complete rein to their love of murder and intimidation." One wouldn't have thought this offered reassurance for the future, but it apparently did. Because the freedpeople understood the consequences of further resistance, Democratic control meant that conflict would end; had Hayes upheld Chamberlain, immediate bloodshed was possible. The House of Representatives, with its Democratic majority, could have cut off army funding and posed other obstacles; as it happened, they tried such measures repeatedly under Hayes. How long could South Carolina have stood as the only Republican state in the region, with militias from neighboring governments poised to invade? While Northerners weren't comfortable with what happened, they would not uphold a government based nearly exclusively on black votes. Abolitionists like Garrison decried it, but few denied the state of national sentiment. Even Chamberlain admitted, "We had lost . . . the sympathy of the North, in some large measure, though we never deserved it so certainly as in 1876 in South Carolina." Northern Republicans would either abandon their Southern allies or lose power. As the former abolitionist firebrand Thomas W. Higginson concluded, "Under the precise circumstances, the President had absolutely no alternative . . . there was nothing else to be done."

To Rutherford B. Hayes the issue never presented itself as surrender. He did not consciously betray black rights; he instead indulged in an optimistic scenario to ease retreat from an impossible situation. He believed that the existing Southern party structure, led by the discredited "carpetbaggers" and dominated by African Americans, was no longer viable. As Frederick Douglass recalled, Hayes told him that "something must be done to break up the race line and the color line in the politics of the South." If the freedmen removed themselves from the bull's-eye of racial hatred, and ratcheted down their demands, the suppressed divisions among native whites over economic policy might reemerge. Blacks could thus obtain a subordinate influence, preferably in alliance with the old Whigs. The Fifteenth Amendment and federal election laws were still on the books, and Democrats had pledged to observe them. Hayes assumed the laws could not be permanently evaded once the immediate provocation lessened. None of it was true, but hopeful people might choose to believe it.

Southern Republicans knew better: white supremacy remained the overriding issue. South Carolina's Senator John Patterson, when he heard the news of Chamberlain's capitulation, erupted in frustration, "I cannot understand what Hayes is driving at; why, he is selling out his party! Talk about dividing the Democratic Party South! Why, it is all moonshine." A nameless black holdout at the Louisiana capital offered a similar prediction: "At first they might treat us well enough, but when they find themselves in undisputed power, we may bid good-bye to any privileges which we now enjoy." He was right, but it took a while. In the meantime Hayes persuaded most national Republicans that the results might be tolerable. Even black spokesmen like John Mercer Langston offered pragmatic support for administration policy. Frederick Douglass accepted a lucrative patronage position under Hayes and passed over the topic in silence in his autobiography. At least the killing would end for a time. But for Northern Republicans the acceptance of the South's terms was provisional, in the expectation that the freedman's legal rights would be respected. As the aging Wendell Phillips observed, "It is hard to imagine any eclipse of public honor so dark as to make his disfranchisement possible." Northerners never quite accepted it when things turned out otherwise.

It took decades for the reality to emerge, for still-cautious redeemers to rearrange matters to their liking. Violence initially declined, a trend furthered by President Hayes's popularity with Southern whites and soothing statements by Democratic leaders.

In South Carolina, Wade Hampton made a moderately enlightened governor, leaving much of low-country governance in
black hands. Higginson, visiting the scene, found "a condition of
outward peace and no conspicuous outrages. . . ." Hayes further
conciliated Southern opinion by withdrawing patronage from
"carpetbaggers," and many of them left the region, depriving
their following of Radical leaders. But by the late 1870s it became
clear that Hayes's hopes of Whiggish conversions to the Republicans were indeed moonshine. While Democrats were happy to
sound responsible, they could not win elections without intimi-
dating the black majority. A continuing steam of election-year
violence resulted in closely contested districts.

The post-"Redemption" settlement was unstable, dependent
on white restraint and black intimidation. For decades Republicans in Congress often overturned contested results, providing a
stream of bad publicity on the national scene, and also black representation. African Americans used their diminishing suffrage
rights to play off one set of white Democrats against the others.
In local elections this was common, but even at the state level
African Americans had success. In Virginia, for example, they
helped dissident agrarian "Readjusters" come to power in the
late 1870s, helping repudiate the huge Democratic state debt and
secure educational funding. And during the Populist revolt of
the 1890s they assisted the insurgent victory in North Carolina.
Both these efforts ended in bloody race riots, which was the pattern whenever blacks made a serious challenge to racial subordination. In a way, Hayes was right: blacks did regain some
influence, so Democrats finally moved to bar the door. By the
turn of the century, in the aftermath of the Populist upsurge,
dominant opinion turned toward an ultimate solution. Disfranchisement laws in the form of poll taxes, literacy tests, and other
means eliminated nearly all black voting in the ex-Confederacy.
Along with these came a host of legal segregation laws and a

style of political discourse that emphasized race supremacy. For the next half-century the Jim Crow South allowed the racial control most whites had sought ever since emancipation.

Given this ultimate trajectory, did Reconstruction matter? Maybe so, one might optimistically conclude. The scale of Reconstruction's challenge to white supremacy, and its catastrophic overthrow, perversely hobbled later opponents of racial equality. The trauma of Reconstruction, trumpeted by turn-of-the-century historians, strengthened the most reactionary forces in Southern life. The legacy reinforced the states' rights Democratic tradition of low taxes and distrust of federal power. Still, the postwar amendments stayed on the books, and there was always the possibility that someday enforcement would resume. Jim Crow meant continual violation of the Constitution, a burden of hypocrisy that proved difficult to sustain. The circumstances left Southern whites striving for perpetual vindication. Redemption also reinforced the tradition of racial lawlessness so evident in lynching and in the periodic reemergence of the Ku Klux Klan. Most fatefully, Reconstruction dangerously persuaded many white Southerners that, when push came to shove, violence to uphold the racial order was morally justified and effective.

Although white supremacist ideas gained influence in the post-Reconstruction North too, the specifics differed. For decades Northerners concluded that direct intervention in Southern affairs was a proven failure. White Americans increasingly accepted a reconciliationist version of the Civil War era that deemphasized racial justice as a motive, as the historian David Blight has argued. Thus when a Democratic Congress finally repealed federal election laws in 1894, and with the subsequent *Plessy v. Ferguson* decision, Northerners acquiesced, and segregation and disfranchisement spread. But however retrograde national sentiment became, it only emboldened further Southern tests of national tolerance. Festival lynchings and urban race riots became notorious around the turn of the century, shocking the entire world. The Klan reemerged as a mass movement, and demagogues like Mississippi's outlandish Theodore Bilbo offended the national decorum. Regional sentiment could never converge because the threat of another Reconstruction engendered abiding extremism.

After the Civil War, African Americans lost the battle for national opinion, perhaps unavoidably given the tentative Northern commitment to racial justice and the limited resources at their command. When a later generation challenged the system, they could build upon the few legal gains to survive Reconstruction, and a better-educated and more prosperous black community brought greater resources to bear. The Great Migration had moved millions of African Americans to the North, where the Fifteenth Amendment actually functioned and anti-racist votes grew. After the war against Nazi racism, a new generation took first to the courts and then to the streets. This time a telegenic leadership and the presence of mass media built a national consensus behind civil rights, eventually encompassing many white Southerners. Martin Luther King and his nonviolent comrades provoked their opponents into catastrophic overreaction. Again and again, at places like Birmingham and Selma, racist violence horrified the nation, and the world. The likes of Bull Connor and George Wallace had learned the lesson of Reconstruction all too well, and in the end, it did them in.

What, then, to conclude about the first attempt to secure basic civil rights? This book has in some respects been critical of Republican leaders. The Reconstruction governments had real problems, some avoidable. Republicans presented themselves in ways that compromised their cause before the national audience. Still, Northern "Radicalism" was an outgrowth of the egalitarian passions of the war, and the realities of Republican rule in Grant's America were unlikely to inspire continued idealistic devotion. Other issues were bound to reemerge and sap the commitment to racial equality. If Republican leaders failed to sustain national resolve, probably nothing would have done so indefinitely in the face of such powerful resistance. Thus, ultimately, we come back to the issue of how best to remember Reconstruction: as a contest between those who attempted the doomed, but mostly right thing, and those who were doing the very wrong thing and prevailed. But only for a time.

A Note on Sources

In briefly describing the scholarly literature on the Reconstruction Era, one is tempted to refer readers to the works of William A. Dunning and his students, if only to highlight the racist enormities of early twentieth-century historians. The older literature rationalized black disfranchisement and Jim Crow, and sometimes even lynching. Think of themes of the silent film *Birth of a Nation*, repeated in various states with footnotes. Small wonder that historical scholarship took a revisionist turn, anticipated in some respects by W. E. B. Du Bois's *Black Reconstruction in America* (New York, 1935). The modern literature dates from after mid-century, beginning with John Hope Franklin's *Reconstruction: After the Civil War* (Chicago, 1961) and Kenneth M. Stampp's *Era of Reconstruction: 1865–1877* (New York, 1965). Revisionists quickly swept the field, erasing half a century of racist dominance of academic scholarship. Given the dramatic backdrop of the 1960s, an implicit analogy with the civil rights struggle animated writing on Reconstruction. The tone of political engagement is manifest; during the 1970s, Radical Republicans were primarily criticized for not being radical enough.

Since that time the rise of social history has also influenced all aspects of Southern history. Major 1970s interpretations of slavery, by Eugene Genovese, Lawrence Levine, Herbert Gutman, and others, transformed our thinking about the evolution of the African-American community. Leon Litwack's *Been in the Storm So Long: The Aftermath of Slavery* (New York, 1979) is probably the most prominent of the works addressing emancipation. Also influential in the direction of the field have been the numerous edited volumes of *Freedom: A Documentary History of Emancipation* (New York, 1982–) by Ira Berlin and Leslie Rowland. The scholars associated with the project generally envision popular politics as growing out of the postwar plantation struggle. With respect to the white population, Steven Hahn's *The Roots of Southern Populism: Yeoman Farmers and the Transformation of the Georgia Upcountry, 1850–1890* (New York, 1983), despite criticism, remains the landmark work on the social evolution of the upland South.

The contemporary literature on Reconstruction politics is anchored by several broad interpretations dating to the 1980s. The first is Michael Perman's *The Road to Redemption: Southern Politics, 1869–1879* (New York, 1984), the most influential study of partisan politics and factionalism, especially with reference to the eventual victors. The eclipse of Whiggish moderation by Democratic racial extremists is well described here, and the book nicely incorporates eleven state histories into a broad interpretation of the region's politics. The role of economic development in this process is also an important part of Perman's story. His earlier *Reunion Without Compromise: The South and Reconstruction, 1861–1868* (Oxford and New York, 1973) is perceptive too, though the interpretation is distinct.

The leading figure in Reconstruction scholarship is Eric Foner. His *Nothing But Freedom: Emancipation and Its Legacy* (Baton Rouge, 1983) is a short but effective comparison with other post-emancipation societies. The emphasis on the crucial role of black enfranchisement in the evolution of plantation agriculture anticipates his magnum opus, *Reconstruction: America's Unfinished Revolution, 1863–1877* (New York, 1988). To an unusual extent, this book remains the standard account, its influence augmented by a popular abridgment, *A Short History of Reconstruction* (New York, 1993), and the biographical compendium *Freedom's Lawmakers: A Directory of Black Officeholders During Reconstruction* (Baton Rouge, 1996). Foner's work incorporates the social history of emancipation and the plantation labor struggle into the political narrative, which explains its lasting appeal. Nearly twenty years after publication, *Reconstruction* remains the outstanding synthesis of revisionist scholarship on emancipation and politics.

Pursuing different insights, some political historians have examined topics deemphasized in the revisionist literature, which has tended toward rehabilitation of the Republicans. J. Mills Thornton's illuminating study of Republican tax policy, "Fiscal Policy and the Failure of Radical Reconstruction in the Lower South," and Lawrence N. Powell, "The Politics of Livelihood: Carpetbaggers in the Deep South," both follow this heterodox line of thought. Both appeared in J. Morgan Kousser and James M. McPherson, eds., *Region, Race and Reconstruction: Essays in Honor of C. Vann Woodward* (New York, 1982). Similarly, Mark W. Summer's *Railroads, Reconstruction, and the Gospel of Prosperity* (Princeton, 1984) examines the Republican railroad program and its various ills. He has also undertaken a number of nuts-and-bolts studies of the political process, among them *The Era of Good Stealings* (New York, 1993). His forthcoming work on political paranoia pursues an underexplored aspect of Reconstruction.

On national politics there are any number of examinations of the federal retreat from Reconstruction. Still excellent is Terry Seip, *The South Returns to Congress: Men, Economic Measures, and Intersectional Relationships, 1868–1879* (Baton Rouge, 1983). Andrew Johnson has inspired a small shelf of books, many dating to the 1960s, but his reputation remains bleak. Representative is Eric McKitrick, *Andrew Johnson and Reconstruction* (Chicago, 1960). For President Grant, see Brooks Simpson, *Let Us Have Peace: Ulysses S. Grant and the Politics of Reconstruction* (Chapel Hill, 1991) and *The Reconstruction Presidents* (Lawrence, Kans., 1998). The modern study of Hayes is Ari Hoogenboom, *Rutherford B. Hayes: Warrior and President* (Lawrence, Kans., 1995).

Many specialized examinations of Reconstruction political topics have appeared. The best case study of the Freedmen's Bureau is Paul A. Cimbala, *Under the Guardianship of the Nation: The Freedmen's Bureau and the Reconstruction of Georgia, 1865–1870* (Athens, Ga., 1997). Richard H. Abbott's *For Free Press and Equal Rights: Republican Newspapers in the Reconstruction South* (Athens, Ga., 2004) offers a pragmatic look at an aspect of Republican rule. Lawrence N. Powell's *New Masters: Northern Planters During the Civil War and Reconstruction* (New Haven, 1980) remains the crucial work on the background of Northern political newcomers. Also quite accessible is Richard N. Current's group biography, *Those Terrible Carpetbaggers: A Reinterpretation* (Oxford and New York, 1989). On the Klan, Allen Trelease's *White Terror: The Ku Klux Klan and Southern Reconstruction* (New York, 1971) surprisingly remains the best overview of this crucial topic. Also insightful is George Rable's *But There Was No Peace: The Role of Violence in the Politics of Reconstruction* (Athens, Ga., 1984). On the related issue of Northern opinion, especially on evolving attitudes on race and class, see Heather Cox Richardson, *The Death of Reconstruction: Race, Labor, and Politics in the Post–Civil War North, 1865–1901* (Cambridge, Mass., 2001).

Of the histories of the era in the various states, several date to the Dunning school and are marred by outmoded racial assumptions. While there are several modern state studies, William C. Harris's *The Day of the Carpetbagger: Republican Reconstruction in Mississippi* (Baton Rouge, 1979) prominent among them, more specialized studies have predominated. The field has been influenced by numerous works drawing on the social history literature. Thomas Holt's *Black Over White: Negro Political Leadership in South Carolina* (Urbana, 1977) remains insightful on the social origins of black politics, augmented by Richard Zuceck's study of terrorist violence as politics, *State of Rebellion: Reconstruction in South Carolina* (Columbia, S.C., 1996). And Christopher Waldrep's quantitative study of the Vicksburg area, *Roots of Disorder: Race and Criminal Justice in the American South, 1817–1880* (Urbana, 1998), is unusual in its emphasis on law enforcement in local context.

There are also a number of well-researched local studies of postbellum plantation evolution. Among these are Joseph Reidy's *From Slavery to Agrarian Capitalism in the Cotton Plantation South: Central Georgia, 1800–1880* (Chapel Hill, 1992). Also, Julie Saville's examination of grassroots politics, *The Work of Reconstruction: From Slave to Wage Laborer in South Carolina* (New York, 1994), and John Rodrigue's *Reconstruction in the Cane Fields: From Slavery to Free Labor in Louisiana's Sugar Parishes, 1862–1870* (Baton Rouge, 2001), look at different regional variants. Susan O'Donovan's forthcoming *Becoming Free in the Cotton South* (Cambridge, Mass., 2007) does likewise for southwestern Georgia but focuses on the social implications of freedwomen's labor. Finally, Steven Hahn's *A Nation Under Our Feet: Black Political Struggles in the Rural South, from Slavery to the Great Migration* (Cambridge, Mass., 2003) offers a broad regional interpretation of the plantation struggle, emphasizing collective self-determination.

The revisionist emphasis on race in Reconstruction often overshadowed other aspects of the era. Jane Turner Censer, *The Reconstruction of White Southern Womanhood* (Baton Rouge, 2003), examines a group surprisingly understudied in recent decades, women of the planter class. For a lively rethinking of the legal impact of Reconstruction on gender politics, see Laura Edwards, *Gendered Strife and Confusion: The Political Culture of Reconstruction* (Urbana, 1997) and Peter W. Bardaglio, *Reconstructing the Household: Families, Sex and the Law in the Nineteenth-Century South* (Chapel Hill, 1995). The religious history of the era, and its wider political implications, has also received fresh interest. Among the more important works is Reginald F. Hildebrand, *The Times Were Strange and Stirring: Methodist Preachers and the Crisis of Emancipation* (Durham, N.C., 1995). Daniel W. Stowell, *Rebuilding Zion: The Religious Reconstruction of the South* (New York, 1998), is the best study of denominational rivalries and Reconstruction politics. More broadly, Edward Blum, *Reforging the White Republic: Race, Religion, and American Nationalism* (Baton Rouge, 2005), is excellent on the wider themes of American racial thought.

For recent historiographic essays on the literature, see Thomas J. Brown, ed., *Reconstructions: New Perspectives on the Postbellum United States* (Oxford and New York, 2006). Finally, I might refer readers to my own work, on which I drew liberally for this book's examples. *The Union League Movement in the Deep South: Politics and Social Change in Reconstruction* (Baton Rouge and London, 1989) examines the politicization of the freedpeople and its influence on plantation agriculture, especially the emergence of sharecropping in cotton. "The Ku Klux Klan: Property Crime and the Plantation System in Reconstruction Alabama," *Agricultural History* (Spring 1997: 186–206), examines the theft issue and the social composition of the terrorist movement. And *Urban Emancipation: Popular Politics in Reconstruction Mobile, 1860–1890* (Baton Rouge and London, 2002) explores black intraracial class tensions and Republican factionalism in the context of rural migration to the region's cities.

Index

A NOTE ON THE AUTHOR

Michael Fitzgerald was born in Chicago, grew up in Los Angeles, and studied at the University of California, Los Angeles, where he received a Ph.D. in history. He has written widely on aspects of Reconstruction, including *Urban Emancipation* and *The Union League Movement in the Deep South*. Mr. Fitzgerald is now professor of history at St. Olaf College and lives in Northfield, Minnesota, with his wife, the historian Judy Kutulas, and their two sons.